IN THEIR
OWN WORDS

Voices From the Middle Passage

IN THEIR OWN WORDS

Voices From the Middle Passage

Edited by
A.J. WILLIAMS-MYERS

Africa World Press, Inc.

P.O. Box 1892
Trenton, NJ 08607

P.O. Box 48
Asmara, ERITREA

Africa World Press, Inc.

P.O. Box 1892
Trenton, NJ 08607

P.O. Box 48
Asmara, ERITREA

Cover artwork: Michael A. Hobbs
Cover and book design: Dapo Ojo-Ade

Library of Congress Cataloging-in-Publication Data

In their own words– voices from the middle passage students as surrogates to the terrorism down in the hold of a slave ship crossing the Atlantic ocean : an introductory reader / edited by A. J. Williams-Myers.
p. cm.   Includes bibliographical references.
ISBN 1-59221-696-X (hard cover) -- ISBN 1-59221-697-8 (pbk.)
1. Slave trade–Africa–History. 2. Terrorism–Africa–History. I. Williams-Myers, Albert James, 1939-
HT1322.I5 2009
306.3′62096–dc22
2009012099

Contents

PART III – A SHARD OF EVIDENCE:
A PAGE FROM HIS DIARY (PIERRE DUSABLE)

PART IV – A SHARD OF EVIDENCE:
A PAGE FROM HIS DIARY (PIERRE TOUSSAINT)

PART V – UP FROM THE DEPTHS:
A REFLECTIVE VOICE

List of Illustrations

Acknowledgements

Due consideration and admiration are extended to the students who gave voice to *the many thousand gone* as well as those who shared their reactions to the gripping realism evident in the recreation of those voices by their peers. Recognition as well is extend to my sister-in-law, Deanne Morizono Myers for her gracious contributions in assisting students in my Historical Terrorism and Race and Racism classes with human tragedy and personal grief. Ms. Myers unselfishly traveled across the country from San Francisco, California to New Paltz, New York to ensure not only the success of the student-teacher project but as well to share her family's tragic encounter with Japanese internment during World War II.

The success of the project as well is due to the college's Instructional Resources Center for technical input with audiovisual during classroom time. Special thanks go to Linda K. Smith, Instructional Technology Coordinator and her staff for the reproduction and electronic transmission of the book's stunning imagery of the Atlantic trade era in humans.

Finally, I wish to acknowledge the powerful insight of my publisher, Kassahun Checole, who saw the educational value in the project as a means to enhance student, and the general public's, comprehension and empathy of a human tragedy that spanned more than three centuries. And it is to his Senior Editor/Editorial Coordinator, Damola Ifaturoti, whom I salute for his patience, direction, and professionalism that carried the project to this successful reawakening to the voices of *the many thousands gone*.

INTRODUCTION: A HIDDEN THREAD OF AMERICAN HISTORY – TERRORISM

Understanding a Hidden Thread of American History – Terrorism

In the wake of 9/11 Americans scurried to make sense out of a terrible human tragedy as well as deal with the word terrorism in terms of its shattering entrance into our daily use of English. On some college campuses, professors put together courses of study that examined either a historical legacy of such violence or that of images of terrorism in a more contemporary world. On the campus of the State University of New York at New Paltz, in the Black Studies Department, I designed the course, "Historical Terrorism Directed at African Americans and Native Americans." It passed the college's Curriculum Committee and was taught for the first time in the Fall Semester of 2006 with an initial enrollment of thirty-three students. Although the nation in post-9/11 found itself in the grip of a worldwide terrorist threat, I design the course, and the Central Committee approved it, to ensure that our students not forget that in this democracy of ours there is a thread of terrorism that has confronted two segments of the country's population since its inception. In the words of one of my students terrorism for those two "has been 24/7".

The course took a historical perspective in its topical examination of the violent encounters between whites and red as well as those between whites and black. Each topic demonstrated the spiraling nature of terrorism in its homegrown version, pointing out its long range impact into the 20th century, and indicating as well that impact on the lives of both Asian and Latino Americans. As the course progressed through the semester, students, through written, visual, and oral exercises, slowly began to grow accustom to the reality of the existence of a historical legacy of a homegrown version of terrorism. For many of them this was initially a difficult challenge because the word terrorism was simply not in their curricular vocabulary when it came to United States History. That history is a series of historical events that depict the growth of an American people spreading a democratic way of life from the Atlantic to the Pacific. Slavery and the encounter with Native Americans are handled with kid gloves.

It was the final exercise of the semester that put the students in a situation of feeling the touch of the long arm of terrorism, reaching out to touch them across a time barrier. The exercise was the viewing of the film, *The Middle Passage*, with each student writing a reaction (on the spot) of what they observed.[1] Each was to put him/herself in the position of the Africans down in the hold of the slave ship chained to its superstructure. They had to envision the terror the Africans were confronted with as they lay in their own body excretions and that of others, with rats scurrying over them and eating at the dead, and the living, while at night having to listen to the moans of the sick, dying, and the cries from the upper decks of women and children being raped by the ship's white crew. It was like psycho-drama: being able not only to understand the unknown but as well to exorcise its nebulous, frightening psychic imagery. In the book students' reactions are introduced only by their first names or with an African alias.

In Their Own Words is a gripping collection of personal reactions to *The Middle Passage* by those who give voice to "the many thousands gone" but were unable to tell the world the horrors to which they were subjected. Voices that

---

[1] HBO Films: Kreol Production and Raphia Films (2005). Narrated by Djimon Hounson and written by Walter Mosley

were once silenced by death while still on board, devour by the schools of ravenous sharks that shadowed the ships, and/or were pulled below the surface of the waters by the mighty swirls of the Atlantic Ocean in centuries past, now reach out to us across that time barrier, having been given expression by students of the twenty-first century in their own words.

Please read and feel the terror that haunted every slave ship that traversed the Middle Passage in the era of the Atlantic slave trade. Be a witness to a reawakening!

A.J. Williams-Myers
New Paltz, New York
2 January 2007

PART I – THE MIDDLE PASSAGE: A SYNOPTIC OVERVIEW

The Middle Passage:
A Synoptic Overview

It was of long duration, monumental in proportions, and one of the most heinous crimes against humanity: it was the uprooting, brutalization, and forced migration of approximately (for some somewhat conservative) twelve to fifteen million Africans across the Atlantic Ocean to various capital-accumulating, economic schemes put in place in the Americas by Europeans.[1] The crime of capturing, buying, and transporting human cargo thousand of miles from the victims' homelands stretched through time from the middle of the fifteenth century to the middle of the nineteenth century. During those centuries the Atlantic voyage has been characterized as the holocaust of an African awakening given the horrors the victims were confronted with cramped in limited, unsanitary space deep in the bowels of slavers. As a result the mortality rate for male, female and children was staggering. On any one voyage, the death rate could be as low as 9.1 percent to as high as 20 percent or more.[2]

The high mortality rate, exasperated by unhealthy

---

[1] Philip D. Curtin, *The Atlantic Slave Trade: A Census* (Madison: University of Wisconsin Press, 1969); W.E.B. DuBois, *The Suppression of the African Slave Trade to the United States of America*, 1636-1870 (Reprint, Baton Rouge: Louisiana State University Press, 1969); David Eltis, et al., eds., *The Trans-Atlantic Slave Trade: A Database on CD-ROM*, 1999; Joseph E. Inikori, "Measuring the Unmeasured Hazards of the Atlantic Slave Trade: Documents Relating to the British Trade." *Revue Francaise d'Histoire d'Outre-Mer*, 83, no. 312 (1996): 53-92.

[2] Cf. Curtin, Ibid; Herbert S. Klein, *The Middle Passage Comparative Studies in the Atlantic Slave Trade* (Princeton: Princeton University Press, 1978): 64-65.

conditions down in a ship's hold, and further compounded by the presence of communicable diseases that infected not only the human cargo but the ship's European crew as well, were further enhanced by food shortages. The slaver *Zong* in 1783 with four hundred Africans down in its hold, and with rations dwindling fast, the captain, concerned with preventing economic failure and aware that insurance would cover loses, made the decision to "throw the sickest slaves overboard alive." In this fashion, 130 live Africans were sacrificed for the sake of financial gain.[3] "Violence, [therefore,] lay at the heart of the slave ship," from the captain who terrorized not only the Africans but the crew as well, to the crew whose fear spilled over into sadistic acts directed at the human cargo, and among the Africans given the tight space and the deteriorating conditions below deck as a voyage progressed through the Middle Passage.[4]

In the Middle Passage "the slave ship [like the *Zong*] was a linchpin [to the rapid growth of an] Atlantic system of capital and labor".[5] Despite the fact that the captain of the *Zong* "murdered" 130 Africans, and given that the ship had exceeded its carrying capacity, the balance of 270 meant a capital gain for the ship's investors. The most infamous slave ship in the Middle Passage that more than once exceeded its carrying capacity was the British ship the *Brookes*. Built in 1781 to carry a little over 300 Africans, the *Brookes* was infamously known for exceeding that by an additional 300. In 1785-86 she carried a staggering count of 740, with "no place capable of holding a single person from one end of the vessel to the other…left unoccupied".[6] For

---

[3] Eric Robert Taylor, *If We Must Die Shipboard Insurrections in the Era of the Atlantic Slave Trade*, (Baton Rouge: Louisiana State University Press 2006): 31-32.

[4] Marcus Rediker, *The Slave Ship A Human History* (Viking, 2007): 260-61.

[5] Ibid, 348.

over a quarter of a century the *Brookes* made ten successful voyages to Africa and back. Out of a total of 5,163 Africans purchased, the ship safely delivered 4,559 to buyers.

The prime specimen for the Atlantic crossing, or what the Portuguese called *peca de India*, was a male or female above the age of twelve but always between fifteen and forty years of age. Yet invariably those younger than twelve ended up in the slave-catcher's net.

That which is missing from most literature on the Middle Passage is the African voice in terms of her or his experience on that Atlantic crossing, that holocaust of an awakening for Africans. Except for a few first-person accounts like those of Ottobah Cugoano and Olaudah Equiano, the voice that is heard is that of the Africans' captors, whites.[7] They, as one author put it, "were the chroniclers of the slave trade."[8] The African voice, therefore, because of this "is silenced in the historical record."[9] In order for us in the present century to fathom the pain and horror of the Middle Passage, it has been a resort to literature that affords us that view and voice through their eyes, thus a reason for this introductory reader. The following quote is a view through their eyes, and is from Basil Davidson's *The African Slave Trade* of an Englishman named simply Walsh. Walsh, in 1829, while on the British patrol ship, *North Star*, which had sat sail from a Brazilian port, witnessed the capture of an illegal slaver with a cargo of 505 men and women, and went on board to view the

---

[6] Ibid., 339.
[7] Cf. Quobna Ottobah Cugoano, *Thoughts and Sentiments on the Evil of Slavery and Other Writings*, edited by Vincent Carretta (Athens: University of Georgia Press, 1999); Olaudah Equiano, *Equiano's Travels: The Interesting Narrative of the Life of Olaudah Equiano or Gustavus Vassa, the African* (Edited by Paul Edwards, 1789. Reprint in 1996).
[8] Taylor, op. cit., 11.
[9] Ibid., 12.

conditions. Before capture the ship's crew had thrown 55 members of the cargo overboard. In Walsh words:

"[...these slaves] were all enclosed under grated hatchways, between decks. The space was so low that they sat between each others' legs, and stowed so close together, that there was no possibility of lying down, or at all changing their position, by night or by day. As they belonged to, and were shipped on account of different individuals, they were all branded like sheep, with the owners' marks of different forms. These were impressed under their breasts, or on their arms, and, as the mate informed me with perfect indifference, burnt with a red hot iron.[10]

The violence and inhumanity perpetrated by the ship's crew upon the African captives, reverberated throughout the Atlantic World and across the centuries searing the soul and conscience of victims and victimizers. The Middle Passage (a vortex of inhumanity) was the crucible out of which rose the ideology of racism that blinded those of European descent to the interconnectedness of the human family. With respect to this crucible in terms of race relations, one author wrote:

Here, on the Atlantic crossing, was forged the essential relations between black and white which survived long after the ending of the Atlantic slave trade itself. The experiences of the crossing were dominated by violence. Indeed, the whole system was violent in its essence.[11]

---

[10] Basil Davison, *The African Slave Trade Precolonial History 1450-1850* (Boston, 1961): xv-xvi. For a general look at the Atlantic slave trade and its controversies see David Northrup, ed., *The Atlantic Slave Trade* (D.C. Heath and company: Toronto, 1994).
[11] James Walvin, *Questioning Slavery* (Routledge: New York, 1996): 51.

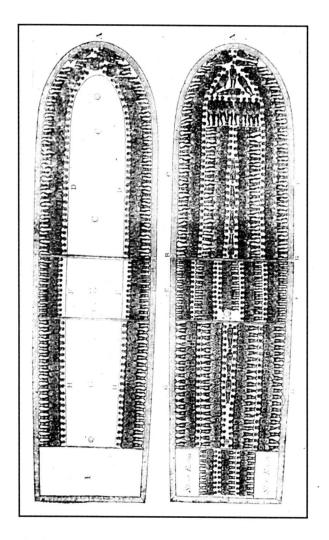

British slave ship, the *Brookes of Liverpool* – cross section of ship showing how African captives were stored below deck in an effort to maximize space and increase profits (From Clarkson's *Abstract of the Evidence*, 1791).

PART II – A SHARD OF EVIDENCE: A PAGE FROM HIS DIARY (FRANCOIS NUNET)

A Shard of Evidence:
A Page from His Diary

17 January 1801 – Seaman Second Class, Francois Nunet aboard the *Henri Real IV*

We are three weeks out from that god forsaken, pestilent-ridden place called Abomme in the Niger Delta. The ship's hold is filled beyond capacity, six hundred of those wretched creatures in a ship built to carry around three hundred. The captain says it's to ensure that when we reach New Orleans on the Mississippi and then on to Martinique in the Caribbean, there will be at least two thirds of the cargo left for a decent profit for the ship's investors. Me, I don't care about profit at this time, I'm sick…been sick for the last week…and I believe I'm going to die on this ship.

The weather is caught in the grip of the devil's blow. The sea has not calmed down, and like yesterday and all night the ship is being battered with giant waves that toss it about like a piece of flotsam: listing to starboard then to port, and with its bow locked in oncoming waves as if to be engulfed and consumed by the sea. I can still hear the cries from below as the human cargo is tossed relentlessly about while chained to the boat and one another. None of the crew has been down in the hold yet. It's got to be a horrendous sight, and with many, I am sure, dead from strangulation and/or trauma from head and body wounds as a result of the violent nature of the ship's abrupt movements in the turbulent waters.

All of this only aggravates my sickness which crept up from among those poor souls chained below in the hold riddled with disease. I have been unable to control

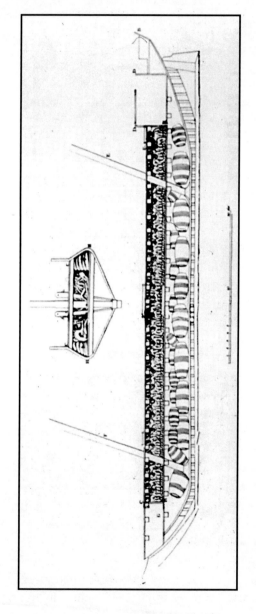

Spanish slave Schooner, *Josefa Maracayera* – cross section with African captives below deck and ship's water supply in barrels used as ballast.

my bowels, and my body is racked with fever. I cannot get enough water in me, and the smell of the ship's meals only makes me nauseous. I am whiter than white...I am a ghost. Like many of those lost souls below I am limited to this upper bunk – in a way my tomb as the lower decks down in the hold are their tomb. Crew members fear me and avoid contact, letting the African cabin boy tend to my needs. I know I'm dying...

Although it was a rough night I could still hear the sounds of crew members in nearby cabins having their way with the African women and children brought up from below deck. I can't remember when I've had a woman last but it doesn't matter now, my body weakens while they violate the innocence of the children and women... I am dying.

18 January 1801 – Seaman Second Class Francois Nunet, aboard the *Henri Real IV*

The weather has calmed and the ship rides the churn of the sea swells like the well built ship that she is. The cries have subsided from below, and the moans are muffled by the sounds coming from the ship and sea caught in a watery minuet. The cries of the women and children are no longer heard. They are back down below with scarred souls. Crew members have been down in the hold, and I can hear the splash of the dead being tossed overboard. The sharks are agitated as they bang the sides of the ship in their furious feast of the offerings. I wonder...is that to be my ending?

I lay here in my own body fluids, much weaker than yesterday and closer to death. My stool and urine are laced with blood, so I must be hemorrhaging internally. The cabin boy does not come for they say he was swept overboard by a huge wave last night while dumping the

captain's night soil bucket. *Another thousand gone...*
I am being lulled into a deep but pleasant sleep. Pain slips all so slowly from my body, and the most brilliant light begins to come aglow around me – I sink into unconsciousness...

Rachel

I stand here with others on the water's edge waiting to be taken aboard large sailing boats. While we wait, white ones burn our skin with red hot irons to mark us as property. They shackle our feet and wrists, and while urging us to move ahead to get into the launches that will take us out to the ship to board, they use whips on us, sparing no one, not even the very little children. We board the giant boat very reluctantly knowing that the Africa we see over our shoulders as we are led through the hatch down into the ship's hold will never be seen again.

Below deck and after a few days out from land, our bodies begin to sweat profusely from the stifling heat. We are chained in unsanitary conditions, and human waste and vermin of all kind simply increase our chances of being exposed to disease epidemics. Some Africans are already beginning to show the first signs of life-threatening illnesses. The whites come among us but hurry to complete their tasks and retreat back to the above decks. They cover their faces with linen to avoid having to breathe the horrible, deadly smells that we are unable to avoid. When the hatch is closed, and it is night, the darkness is overwhelming, but with the first sign of daybreak beans of light penetrate the dark allowing one to readjust to a world that is up and down.

Although we were from different clans and spoke different languages, our common, deplorable conditions down in the hold link us to a sense of community, although tenuous and momentarily. As one, we begin to see that the pale foreigners are a restless group. They do not know how to sit still and be in harmony with the Universe. We ponder the meaning behind this human characteristic. Does it speak to the need to dehumanize us the way they do? What of the homeland from which they come…are they all restless like this, all the time?

Their need to dehumanize us can be seen in the unsanitary conditions we are subjected to down in the hold of this ship. It is rat infested, sickness and diseases rack our bodies, with the sick and weak unable to control the expelling of body waste, thus littering the planks of the deck with excretion. At night these white men come among the women to select us for use as unwilling sexual partners above deck. They steal our innocence and that of the children as well. Many bodies are already scarred from the incessant whippings, now the white ones have begun to scar the soul.

I feel I will die on this ship and not be remembered because the family will never receive my bones. I am at a loss as to what had I done to bring this anger down on me. Uncontrollable fear continues to shake the little self-control I have left. Death seems like the only way to be free from these unendurable days. Some of us commit suicide, hoping to reach the holy spirits and get away from these horrid circumstances. Those who are able to survive feel a slight glimmer of hope with the realization that the white foreigners fear us. This hope gives strength and counteracts the ever present option of suicide. We cling to hope…and live another day…

*   *   *

Takeya

Strangers, the color of death awaken me in the middle of the night. I can hear them clump down the steps into the hold which is the sound of their hunger for innocence. They take two this time: a boy and a girl. As they unshackle them with a savage look in their eyes, I feel ashamed. Ashamed because they take our young and pure, and damage their bodies by raping them; filling them with sin, washing all purity. I am ashamed again because I wish it were I that was unshackled.

I have been caged like an animal, not free to roam for days now. I haven't seen sunlight in two days. As I lay on the top shelf, I can see the blood from my womb drip onto the black body under me. I have no way to take care of my menstrual cycle. As the youth above me scream to our god for help, I close my eyes in hopes that this will be a nightmare that I awaken from tomorrow.

As daylight hits, the first sight I see are rats. The rodents bite and tear around my shackled body. They roam this hole of blackness following the putrid smell of feces, vomit and sweat in hopes to find food. Of all these foul odors, one is distinct – the smell of death. After the pale strangers throw the bodies of our lifeless men overboard, they return below to tell us that it is time to dance. Those who are strong enough to walk, slowly trudge to the top deck. Welcome by sunlight we dance to our gods.

After the dance is over we begin to retreat back down below to the shallow darkness of the hold. Before fully reaching the pit of the hold, I look back to see the men and women that decided to free their souls of the white man's captivity – they jump to their deaths into the swirling sea. This is a constant repeat of the tragedy that occurs day after day.

The white beasts bear fear in their eyes as they push us

downstairs back into the hold toting pistols and daggers. A while later as they feed me a handful of grub, I close my eyes and vow to live another day...

* * *

Christina

It's terrifying down here with the living and the dead. The smells are unbearable...the foul smells of those chained below, above and beside me, all trapped in their body secretions. I attempt to understand the different languages I hear, somewhat uncomfortable knowing that we are all foreigners thrown into this hold together. What did we do to offend the gods to end up like this? Who are these white foreigners...these pale ones?

I am frightened of what is next in store for me, be it rape, dying of starvation, some form of sickness, being tossed alive from the ship into the shark infested waters, or just finding myself unable to tolerate the conditions and eventually committing suicide.

Why, why me? Why must I lay here and watch those around me – the living and the dead – be eaten by rats. Some of those who are still alive are so weak that they are defenseless against the attacks of determined, hungry rodents who are attracted by the open, oozing body wounds. They are relentless and everywhere, both at night and during the day. I feel them brush past me at night, and have on occasion awaken with one or two perched on my right hip and with their red, beady eyes looking directly into mine as if to say *it wont be long*...

I lay here chained to the ship, missing my homeland and my people from whom I have been separated and will never see again. The pale ones enter the hold and bring us garbage to eat and, occasionally, dirty water to drink.

Why is this happening? Why do these pale humans treat us this way? What wrong have we done to them to invite this wrath of theirs upon us? What makes them do this to another human of a darker hue? Here I lay locked in rusty chains and being treated far worst than any animal – why?

The children who are chained like us down here are so young, innocent, and pure. Oh, if we could only break these chains and go to their aid. At night the pale ones come for them to do heinous things to them.

These aliens fear us. I can see it in their eyes. They fear as well the fate of many of us who have died of sickness, so they cover their mouths and nostrils with linen and throw a pungent solution around the hold in a cleansing fashion.

I don't know if I should be happy or sad that I wake tomorrow to another day. And if I do I hope that the ship will have arrived at landfall. Time seems like it is taking eternity to reach land. I want to die yet I want to live. I have been humiliated and torn from all that I know. My body aches. And no doubt there are other women down here who feel such pain as well; many are on their menstrual cycles and perhaps even pregnant with child.

* * *

Kelley

I wait on line and the terror of the unknown consumes me. I'm frozen with fear as cold metal shackles are pounded in place around wrist and ankle. I tremble as a red hot iron brands a foreign symbol onto my skin. Then, like a herd, we are forced into the darkness of the ship's bottom.

Fear consumes my mind as my eyes struggle to accept such blackness. I don't know where we're headed or what horror awaits us. I lay on the hard wooden planks, shackled and sweaty, and the vomit from those shackled around me spills from their mouths onto the deck as they grow sicker from the pitch and roll of the ship in the rough seas. Their sea sickness is enhanced by the many nauseous smells, and all is compounded by the little air that is permitted down in the hold. Rats scurry and move across me, and I cannot move to brush them off. The sound of their nails scratching the floorboards and the crash of the waves against the sides of the ship are the only sounds I hear as I fall asleep.

We are given filthy water to drink and I gulp it readily as it is our only hope for hydration. People are dying – dehydrated, diseased. We are whipped and our wounds weep. People are killing themselves out of desperation and despair; what hope is there to have? The corpses are flung overboard without final rites, and even in death we will be enslaved, our souls doomed to be lost and unable to return to Africa.

With every wave I feel further and further from home and further from hope. Sleep is the only relief, which is stolen many times over with the sailors raping us. I feel like there is nothing left to be taken, we're like beasts beaten and used for any purpose without half the care most animals receive.

When we think things can't be worse, we have a food shortage, and the sailors eat our food. They throw us overboard at the first sign of disease, and we're still alive…

We eventually reach land, and it is not the end of the terror, but a new beginning!

*   *   *

Ashton

I ask the gods…look into my eyes, what do you see? Do you see my hurt and pain? Do you see a person who has been taken from the only place known as home? Tell me what do you see?

As I lay here in the dark, dank endless night it comes to me again as to how I and others ended up down here in the belly of this boat. The captors came to my land beyond the wide, muddy river and burned many of our villages, and in a violently, forceful way took me and my people away chained to one another, marching for days to the big lake with large and small boats upon it. We rested for the night on the shore of that big body of water, but awakened abruptly at the first sign of light and the branding of black bodies began. One by one we followed in line waiting to be the next victim of that red hot iron with its symbol burned into the flesh of our upper arms. When it was my turn I fainted from the excruciating pain that raked my entire body. I came to my senses just as I and others were boarding what they called a ship; and as we were being directed down into the ship's hold I looked back over my shoulder at Africa in the distance, and knew then that I would never, ever see home.

Down in the hold, and as the pale human beings methodically chained us to the inner structure of the ship and to each other, I could feel the ship swaying back and forth, and hear the water slosh up against its sides. First they chained my feet, then my hands, and finally the pale ones chained me to a female to my left and another to my right, and all securely fastened to the ship. There were people above and below me, trapped as beasts in this dark, ungodly rat infested place that would be our prison until the ship reached its destination or we died and were thrown overboard.

So here I lay in the hold of a ship built to carry 300 people but they have packed an additional 300, leaving very little room to stretch or even turn while one lay shackled. There are men and women as well as children, with some still at the breast, and with some women showing signs of pregnancy. We women and children are on a deck closer to the upper deck where the pale ones stay when not down among us, and the men are a deck below us.

The air down here is beginning to feel thick, muggy and hot, almost as if someone had placed a bag over our heads. It is too hot to move, if one really could, so I'll just lay still and wait to see what the new day will bring. It is dark but as my eyes get accustom to it I can make out the shadows of people around me, and at times see the whites of their teeth and eyes. We are engulfed more in darkness than daylight, and when the pale ones open the hatch to the hold to bring us food, the light is so cutting that we initially cover our eyes to avoid the sharp glare.

Unable to move and perform bodily functions in private, I, like all the others chained to this demon of a ship, do our business where we lay. Over time the smells are noxious to humans but are attractions for the relentless vermin that prowl among us in search of edibles: crumbs of gruel that was a meal, the open wounds/sores of the living, and the rotting bodies of the dead not yet removed. The rats are everywhere, perhaps more of them than us... The hold is washed down at times by the pale ones throwing water on us and a fowl-smelling solution onto the floor to wash human excretion and other waste through small slits cut into the baseboards of the hold's walls. In my cramp space I lay waiting to be awakened by a family member from this seemingly, endless nightmare. They don't come, so I remain in its tight grip.

Although constantly chained, there are times that I do get to move about, and that is when I and others are taken up on deck under the sky to dance for the pleasure of the pale ones, to the sounds of their music instruments. As I dance I continue to question what it could have been that I did to bring the wrath of the gods down upon me, to put me in this ungodly situation. The pale ones think they are doing me and others a favor through this exercise of dance. I hate it! I hate the light that shines around us as if something good is going to happen to me. Each time we are brought up here the pale ones use their whips and fists on us as we climb the stairs. It is frightening and painful, and those who can no longer bear the pain and abuse, die a spiritual and physical death and are thrown overboard to be eaten by the school of sharks that constantly follow the ship in search of human prey. Is that to be the fate of us all?

Eventually I learn to dance for the sake of dancing but not for the pleasure of the pale ones but for my pain. I dance to the beat of African drums that come from within me and others, praying all the while as our bodies sway and bob to music that only we can hear. We dance as if in a trance, moving like dark shadows against the lighted sky, until suddenly the pale ones are on to us. But before they can put a stop to the dance, fifteen of the dancers jump overboard to the hungry schools of sharks that tore their bodies to bloody pieces before our very eyes. They preferred the jaws of the sharks to the filth, stench, rats and inhumanity of the pale ones. They are free! *Spirits of the sea, we offer you our bodies, accept them!* Africans believe that death in a place like this ship frees the soul, and that once free it will one day find its way back to Mother Africa.

The pale ones tell us that we will be better off in the New World, but we ponder the meaning of this. As the water beats against the ship we continue to think and pray to the spirits. As we lay in the belly of this ship, I observe those around me with a careful eye for detail. Physically they are chained to the ship in a prostrate position but mentally they fade away from their bodies to be at peace, locked away in an ancestral heaven. For me, I pray each day to be awakened from this endless nightmare …to be free!

The nightmare soon begins to slowly dissipate as I and the others detected fear in the eyes of the pale ones, and it is even there although they possessed weapons and we do not. They fear us. We, who are defenseless, sick, dying, put fear into the pale ones. It is our time, time to take no more. It is time to revolt! Silently we bid out time. We use the time to plan and then to attack when least expected. I know this is the only way I can be free, free from the rats, the horrible conditions and the pain. The hot oil is thrown and you could smell the flesh of the pale ones being burned. With that I, along with other women, and later some men, rush up from below to the ship's deck, out into the brisk, night air. It's my turn, I think to myself as I jump from the ship's railing, hitting the water face first and praying that my people will be free. I give my soul to the gods to take and carry away from this demon ship. Carry it away back home to Africa where I belong.

* * *

Sunday (nine years of age)

Where are Jamal, Isis and Ahmad? I look out over the faces of the other children packed tightly in this space with the awful smells but I can't see them. I look into the face of each in hope against all hope knowing that they never boarded the ship. Jamal and Ahmad, after a week on a yoked-march from our burned-out village, were sold to some Muslim traders trekking north to cross the desert. Every night when the slave caravan rested, I and my sister, five-year old Isis, cried over their loss. There were no others to comfort us... we were alone among many. The raiders killed mother and father, and many of the elderly, and separated family members as they linked us together by wooden clamps to our necks – young and old, women and men – to march us out of the highlands down to the coast. Many of the women had babies still at the breast. The four of us at first were fortunate to have been kept close to one another...until they sold our brother and cousin to the Muslim traders. Isis, weak from exhaustion and hunger, took sick with fever upon our arrival on the beach. She died one day shortly after we were burned on our shoulders. She never let out a scream from the pain, just fainted away dead. They left her body in the shade of a tree covered with palm fronds. I am so alone even though there are so many around me...

Me and another boy about my years, are used to clean up in the captain's deck house, and when needed, along with three or four almost naked, pale-looking cabin boys, work in the galley picking up after those who prepare the food. They cook some of the most horrible-looking food, both for the ship's crew and the Africans chained down below. The galley is difficult to keep clean, rats and field mice everywhere, and the galley men do their personal business in buckets off to the side behind a linen cloth. We eat in the galley from a common bowl, and at times have been fed outside the captain's deck house lashed to one of the long boats. When the sea is disturbed, it is difficult to stand or even walk, and for those of us who have work topside, we as well are lashed together with ropes strung from the yarn.

So far I have been spared the horrors of what the children and women go through each time night falls over the water. Three little girls of about seven, maybe eight, years cling to one another for support and comfort after

their nightly ordeals above deck. They cling, swaying with
the pitch of the ship, eyes that stare out into nothingness, a
shell of that youth they once were...almost the living dead...
I see Isis in them and wish I were big like men back in my
village so that I could protect their innocence from these
pale vultures, these soulless creatures that walk upright,
taking human form but are beast from the underworld
where evil resides. They and other children have lost all
hope of ever believing that they will live out a childhood.
I ask myself that very belief in the form of a question as I
slowly drift off into a restless sleep...and wondering when
daylight breaks whether or not it is my day to suffer the
indignities of the three little girls... I sleep...and my soul
runs off to play with Jamal, Isis, Ahmad and the other
village youngsters among the stalks of corn in the fields
off from the village in sight of the swift flowing, muddy
river. With them I find comfort and companionship...in a
dream.

* * *

Aneisha

As I was being chained and led on to the ship, I knew life
as I had known it would never be the same. They chained
us all together and led us down into the hold of the ship.
Since we were chained in that fashion, together we swayed
and bobbed with the movement of the ship as it edged its
way out into deeper waters. Trapped down in this dark
chamber, I only could conclude that this was genocide in
an attempt to wipe my people out.

Chained in such a position, unable to move about, we
had no choice but to release our body waste onto ourselves
and others. Soon the smell was unbearable and eventually
many grew sick and not long afterward died. Some bodies

lay still chained for days with the smell of rotting flesh further aggravating the unhealthy surroundings, until the pale ones came and took the dead above to toss them into the sea. We could hear the sharks hit the sides of the boat as they fought to devour those thrown overboard.

Imagine us lying there chained with rats nibbling at open wounds on our bodies, and there was nothing we could do because of how we were restrained by the chains. On top of this, imagine how we were being beaten by the pale ones who vented their frustrations upon our helpless and defenseless bodies. As I lay there I wondered what we could have done to them to be treated in such an inhuman fashion. I thought perhaps it was fear. But fear of what... are we not human like them? Yet they treat us as if we were not. They feed us like animals, giving a handful of something that looks like food fit for a pig but, with no other recourse, we eat it. And while we eat they would further vent their anger and frustration upon us with kicks and blows from their fists. I prayed for death!

Many diseases broke out among us, and immediately the pale ones came and unchained those that were diseased, but alive, and took them above to be tossed overboard. We were so often in the dark of the hold that our eyes became accustomed to it. Nighttime was the best for us because at least then we could dream about a life that would be better...

The pale ones would often force us to go up on deck and dance for them still chained together in sets of six or more. This was for their entertainment but it all changed one day while we were in the middle of a dance. At that point we silently together called upon the ancestors for strength, and before the pale ones could react, fifteen Africans, chained in sets, quickly lunged at the ship's railing and flung themselves down into the shark-infested waters.

We prayed for their souls to return to Mother Africa.

The nerve of these pale ones to think that because many of us prefer death to the living death of the ship's hold, that this is why the ship is *cursed*. These pale ones are the cursed, the demons from the depths of hell who beat, rape and murder us. And to think that they say we are not a strong people. To have been able to survive the dreaded Middle Passage is more than sufficient evidence to demonstrate such strength...

* * *

Diego

When did we offend the spirits to have caused them to unleash this abomination upon us? Who are these pale creatures who have rounded up entire villages, placed us in chains and then sent us to the dark bottom of this wretched ship? We watch them pray to a god, giving thanks, asking protection... Is this real? For what act against the gods did we commit to reap this punishment? Has the world as we know it turned upside down? These pale creatures rape our women and children, and they throw our bodies, dead or diseased-ridden but alive, into the ocean. Africa will certainly forget that we ever existed. Perhaps we are to forget Africa and submit to the darkness of our pain and suffering.

The silence, at times, down here is deafening. Where are the sounds of the drums...the voice and songs of the village? What will become of our souls if we cannot connect with our spirits? Certainly the balance of the universe itself will come undone! Cursed are these people! They will feel the repercussions of this act against our humanity for generations to come...

We watch them everyday as they watch us. Something

has occurred to us. We see it in their eyes. We feel it in their chains. We sense it in their guns... They are *afraid*. They fear us. We all gain a sense of strength in this realization. Now, we check for weaknesses...we wait for the right moment...then we will strike. We do not fear death the way they fear us. They do not know that we do not submit to the lie they scream: "die forever". We are Africans, born in a ray of light in the heart of the sun that says "die, but be reborn".

This journey is our death. Those of us who survive are the ones who will undergo a rebirth on the other side, at the end of this journey. It is our children who must not forget us in their memory. A new race will be born out of the scorn that is the foundation of our African nations. We will one day build an army that will shatter the world that is built on our *Deaths*! Justice from the court of humanity will one day rain down on these cursed peoples. Then, one day, our people might be free again.

*   *   *

Darryl

The bowels of the slave ship are filled with Africans from various tribal regions in the hinterland. Although we share very little in languages, we do understand that we are enduring the unendurable. The darkness, disease, despair, sweltering heat, and death all haunt us everyday. Each day is terror in itself but nights are worst. I can hear the dead and sick being unchained and carried up to the main deck to be thrown overboard. At the same time I cannot drown out the sounds of agony and pain of the females being rape by the hairy, pale creatures on the deck above me. It goes on endlessly, night after night...

Shackled to the wooden beans down in the dark, smelly

hold of the ship, we staved off death through prayers and our spirituality. It gives us hope and strength. Through our prayer and meditation we begin to understand that the pale ones who imprisoned us are really afraid of us. The time chained allows us to contemplate our fate and, if possible, to plan for action when the pale ones least expect it. We know that our destiny is in our own hands, if we are to survive, but what is possible against those who have weapons and we none? Some chose suicide while I and others elect to fight back as valiantly as an oppressed, trapped people can, and without fear of death. We want to return to Africa and will do anything to end this terrible nightmare.

Again, our only means of survival is our spirituality. We pray and pray for answers to our dilemmas, and always it points to resistance. In reaching this decision, we are also aware of how weak we are due to disease, malnutrition, and the beatings from the pale ones that are endless. It is decided that the best time to rise up would be within the sight of landfall. We strike…weak…but determined to regain our freedom or die trying.

Our numbers, as we strike, appear smaller than when we were led down into the hold, but our will to live and determination to fight are evident in the look of the pale ones. We fight them with our hands, feet, teeth, and any object we can grasp, even with their own weapons once in our possession. We fight…we die…we fight some more… we die… We fight a fight without end.

* * *

Chatura (She recollects her ordeal)

I was chained to other Africans below deck, men, women and children on the same deck, but there was a deck above me with only women and one below with only men. The first few nights out on the water from Africa I cried for my mother, father, and my sisters and brothers. We all got separated in the frightful rush of things in our village and I have not seen any of them since. I was confused as to what was going on. No one spoke my tongue. We were all foreigners. It would be almost impossible to scheme so that we might free ourselves from these chains that bound us to the inners of this god-forsaken ship. Realizing this, I resigned myself to my plight but continued to wonder why this had become mine and the others' fate, and what would ultimately come of us.

I am deathly afraid of rats or any kind of rodent but I grew accustom to their presence scurrying among us, and viewed them as prisoners as we were. Yet I loathe them for what they are…scavengers whose diet include the flesh of the dead as well as the rancid, runny body wounds of the living, and the fecal matter from the human cargo that litter the wet, slimy deck. The air in the hold was stifling, augmented by the horrible smells of a humanity encased in the bowels of this demon ship.

Those around me died everyday, and with each death I cried and prayed for their souls to be at peace. The more I became aware of death, the more it began to dawn on me that we would never be free again. I contemplated suicide or death by any means that would release me from this living hell. It never came, either up on deck in the salty air or down in the hold among the dead and dying. I thought: was I to survive this hellish journey of the Middle Passage so that the seed of Africa might be planted and harvested in a land in need of truth and salvation?

* * *

Ginell

My heart aches to imagine what it may have been like to be chained along with other suffering Africans. To think of the heat, the putrid smells, the dreadful sounds. I wonder how I would have coped in the midst of so much terror. I close my eyes stinging from emotion and see it – that which "the many thousands gone" encountered, the dreaded Middle Passage.

Stacked below the deck of a slave ship making its way across the Atlantic Ocean, I find myself, along with other nameless bodies, chained down in the darken interior of the slave ship. I am scared and confused as to the massiveness of this large sailing *machine*. Indescribable fear engulfed my body as creatures without color bound me to the ship with those heavy chains. I lay in a very narrow space next to others, and with very little room to turn or sit up. I cry uncontrollably each night.

I feel like cargo as the pale foreigners *package* and *wrap* us hurriedly and roughly in the same manner. I am but *another black body in a sea of dark despair*. Down in the bowels of this dark, wet, foul smelling ship the conditions are unbearable. As I struggle not to give into such an inhuman environment, I inexorably am being consumed by it.

When I have to look into the eyes of these pale foreigners I see cruelty and lust. Restrained as I am, I am defenseless against their attacks. The dark of the hold is pierced by the light of their lanterns as footsteps of the pale ones are heard descending the stairs to my lower deck. I tremble with fear. They come at times for me, for other women, even for the children, and while the men can only listen from below, they have their way with us far into the endless night entombed in this sarcophagus of a ship. Aside from the physical pain and suffering, I can feel my soul dying...dying ever so slowly.

The burning question inside is what have I, and the others, done to our ancestors to end up in this infinite nightmare? We are sick on the outside, throwing up from the noxious smells and the tasteless gruel fed us, and are killed at any sign of disease by being taken above and toss overboard. We who continue to survive need the power of the music, our dance, and ceremonies to bolster the spirits. But instead we are forced to dance to the beat of their meaningless music for their entertainment. When one of us dies either by their hands or through the despair of our own suicide, no funeral ceremony is performed. What will become of our souls?

I lay in my space deep in thought and the idea of death comes to me. Some would say that to take ones life would be a way to end this nightmare yet such a decision would paint the individual as weak. Although I have at times wished for death, I also wish to live another day, perhaps that day will be my awakening from this nightmare. My body pains and my soul longs to be free of this abomination, yet I have resigned myself to wait for that *another day*, and in awakening to regain my lost freedom and humanity. My heart which has grown calloused will soften with each day as I grow stronger, and I will smile again. I know I will!

But how can I think of smiles as I lay here and hear my men being whipped and shot? Or hear the cries of the children, my children, and be a witness to the many deaths occurring around me constantly- how can I think of smiles? How can I think of smiles when I cannot avoid hearing the splash of the body of another one of us – brother or sister – into the ocean?

At this moment my only weapon is prayer. I would pray that those who have died will find their souls back home in Africa; and those still chained down in this hold with me will be strong enough to endure the suffering that is yet to come. In the midst of this terror by now I no longer ask WHY, I whisper in my anguish, WHEN? When will all the suffering of my people end?

As I reopen my eyes, the word WHEN rings in my ears, and I realize we are still asking…I am still asking…

* * *

Jennifer

The darkness at the bottom of the ship that enveloped us only grew darker as the days passed. Although we were from different regions in West Africa, of different peoples with different languages, our captivity made us one. Together we were confronted with the most inhumane and unsanitary conditions to which one individual could subject another. We are chained to the ship and to one another, and exposed to terrible, deadly odors and diseases that stifled the air and racked the bodies of the weak and dying.

Rumors of our fate spread, such as our bodies being eaten by the pale foreigners or offered up to their strange gods to whom they seem to pray but so unlike how we pray to the ancestors. We women are terrorized at night as the foreigners come below to take us above to violate our womanhood. The children are also terrorized in this fashion as well. These pale foreigners can only be emissaries of the devil; how else could they do what they do to the young and innocent… Some of us choose to commit suicide in the belief that our souls will be free and return to Mother Africa, our home. But in our hope against all hope, which is in vain, we resign ourselves to what appears to be fated and begin to feel no more pain. We become numb to the abuse from our tormentors…

The natural joy that children usually possess when at play is no longer there upon their faces. There are only blank stares into nothingness as they sway back and forth with the motion of the ship, all the while wrapped in shock and pain from the endless nights of abuse and rape at the hands of the pale foreigners…children no more…

One thing that cuts the heart the most is that fellow Africans were the ones who captured the majority of us. Our abduction was to satisfy the slave traders. The villages were set on fire in such a way that it was difficult for many of us to escape the raiders. Those that were captured were split into two groups: those that had skills were sent to work for the king, and those who had few skills needed were sold to the slave raiders and ended up down in the hold of this demon ship from the world of the dead.

After having been witnesses to the many of us who were thrown overboard for one reason or another such as having died, contracted a contagious disease or murdered by one of the foreigners, the day came that we decided to strike a blow for our freedom – we rebelled. Many of us were killed by their weapons but we fought; we fought until we could fight no more for what had become to them a losing battle, but for us it was a victorious effort, and the souls of our many heroes hopefully found their way home to Mother Africa… We women were raped repeatedly that night as punishment for the pale ones' loss of fellow crew members and the wounds inflected by us to their bodies.

*   *   *

Esperanza

The waters, the tide, the hate are all sending my body into what feels like a seizure. Replaced with shackles is where my tribal beads used to dangle. If they were still in union with my body, my soul, they would be swaying with the movements of this endless sea. But nothing sways on this ship. Violent torrents of agony are all that moves amongst us. My body though held down by rusty metal, still moves. Moves – it sounds too pleasant a word - …moves are what my body produced when the drums sang blessed beats of Africa. Moving was what my feet did on the soil of our Motherland when we chanted songs of praise and thanked her with our smiling feet. We hear no drums here. Our drums have been replaced by clinking metal and snapping whips. Our voices don't sing for there is no time available in between vomiting and searching for our identity – our voice.

We don't sing for our tears strangle our throats. And when they play their wretched songs, they expect us to dance but above the sounds they produce are the cries and wordless pangs of terror we women and children must endure as our bodies, minds and spirits are penetrated by the slavers' corrupted hands, eyes, mouths, *penis whips*… We are raped – every part of us. And as shadows of light shine through to the lower deck, we realize we too must become shadows; at least you can see shadows. Here on this ship we are not even seen, just one blended, black body to abuse. At least you can see shadows. To set our souls free, we shadow the lining of the sea and the sky that looks down upon our descending bodies, and hope that within them will be preserve our story as our souls transcend this horror. In this way we will fly: our bodies can be eaten by the fish and the fish by the birds that will soar between the sea and the sky back to Mother Africa.

In the midst of our minds and bodies being molested, we see something in the eyes of the oppressors. Despite their position of power, seeping out of their pupils is fear. Our spirits strengthen as a result of the fear we detect they possess. We find further strength in the memories of Mother Africa, of our ancestors. We ask for guidance but our pleas are muffled by our cries, by the diseases that rack our bodies, by the unmerciful rawhide whips that thrash our bare backs into the thickness of the stale, sick air. The boards on which we lay chained are caked with the vomit, sweat, blood, waste and parts of our souls as all spill constantly and profusely from our battered bodies. We women are still robbed of our divinity, the children of their innocence, and our brothers of their dignity.

Each day we are reduced by the many who give in to the mercy of the sea. And the ones that do not meet their freedom through death must carry the message of the Middle Passage deep within the rawhide gashes that cut excruciatingly painful into their backs.

Eventually our story will be told: screamed, sung, and chanted, however the delivery. But one thing is absolute, and that is we will be heard!

*   *   *

Jacob

I became a slave, just another uncivilized man waiting, fearful and confused amidst languages I do not understand. 600 souls stacked into a 300-capacity ship. Sweat, darkness, and filth overwhelm this fear. Why are white people doing this? Except from the cracks of the boat, no light; there is no light. 17 suicides were carried out. I am going to die unless I communicate with others down here in this hold, and with God. We called upon God in prayer.

This humility – dancing in front of a white violinist as they whip us, demonizing our culture, our strength. We are hard: sleeping on just wooden planks chained to the ship, in among the scurrying, hungry rats and smeared with human excrement. The diseases that lurk below, infecting the weak and the strong are our enemies, and the white ones fight them with periodic attempts at cleansing: washing down our area and us with sea water and a sharp smelling solution that sends the rats and other vermin scurrying out of the wake of the wash. But left in such demonic, inhuman conditions, I and others pray for death and the eventual flight of our souls back to Mother Africa and home to our villages on the left bank of the swiftly moving River Niger. The putrid air in the hold engulfs and we are not alive. We are like caged animals. But something greater than us from deep down in our souls urge us to breathe and pray, to pray more and more each day. So we – in the midst of hell – breathe and pray, breathe and pray, putting ourselves into the hands of the ancestors.

Rape – women and children getting violated by old white sailors. If they resist they die. Music they make with their instruments in order for us to dance for their enter-tainment. Again, I wish for death but in remembering the baobob tree back in my village as the symbol of strength and endurance, and feel the spirits of the ancestors move through me I reach for prayer and not death. I am a musician, a drummer, one who makes joy for others. I must live to see that joy upon their faces again. I must strive here in the depths of this darkness of the hold to instill an inner joy within me and to preserve it for that time when I will once again beat out the rhythms of happiness.

I call upon the Oreishas (spirits) and thank God for sending them to follow and comfort us. I cry out in my weakened voice: Take me, bring me to the Oreisha and ease my pain! How do the white ones expect us to survive like this? They think we are transcendent of pain and hunger. To them *we can see no further than the present*.

I am shocked by the false stories of the white captain: *It will be better in the New World* (while we die from exhaustion). And as the first rays of the sun penetrate the cracks of the ship, I pray for strength and that this day is better than the last. The foreigners, we detect, as the day progresses, are afraid of us. They have inferior complexes – they fear us. But why fear...when we are the helpless ones? This gave us strength, strength to conspire and, possibly, revolt...revolt? Yes, revolt, if for anything the children. The white foreigners confuse the children, and make them think that they are less than what they are. The minds of our young ones are affected greatly by this pain and suffering. I am frightened for them but I pray. I feel that we will soon revolt, if not in success at least dying while fighting back. The night is calming and there is solace from the stars – thank you night!

The white sailor dies and they pray! They honor Mary and her son, but how, why such merciless violence while praying to their God? What about the Africans they kill daily? The Africans believe in a God too, the one, true God! The white sailors need to come to a realization of this African belief in the true God. The white foreigners are upsetting the order of the Universe by throwing live people overboard into the sea without a funeral ceremony. This is sin. This is barbaric and evil. We will be reborn. So we revolt, we fight, and are free, if only for a moment...a new man, a new race...

*   *   *

Cape Coast Castle, 1806 with slave ships at anchor awaiting human cargo (Peabody Museum, Salem, Mass.).

PART III – A Shard of Evidence:
A page from his Diary Pierre DuSable)

A Shard of Evidence:
A Page from His Diary

13 February 1801 – Boatswain, Pierre DuSable, aboard the *Henri Real IV*

Monsieur Capitan!, I cry out from the lower bunk in the officers' quarters in hopes of getting a response. But there is none. I call for help in my distress as my body, racked with fever and ulcerating sores that cover my face and upper torso, shivers in the moist heat of the cabin. I have come down with one of those diseases that are rampant among the Africans in the hold. Could be pox or maybe the flux, but whatever it is I need help. Yet no one comes to the sound of my distressed voice.

The sea is turbulent today and the ship is being tossed about like tree limbs caught in a violent wind storm that will soon break and fall to the ground as we in this ship might do to the bottom of the ocean. Though I am weakened by the disease I managed to strap myself securely in the bunk. The other night I was tossed about so violently by the ship's movements that the vision in my left eye is somewhat impaired. *Monsieur Capitan!*, I cry out again. Why, I ask, did I sign on for this trip? Aren't I too old for this kind of adventure…should I not be home in Leon with my grandchildren? Will I ever see them again? As I now, in the throes of death, question the wisdom of it all. Haven't I taken this voyage enough times to have known that sooner or later the cards are staked against you? How many times or how long must a man stay at the wheel to finally know that the house always wins…that l'mer (sea) will have its way with those who continue to tempt fate?

I lay horrified, shivering with droplets of cold sweat that drenched my garments. Very few of my men, if any, call for me or come to inquire of my condition. They are afraid. My immediate subordinate has assumed responsibility for the deck crew. The French cabin boy who tended my needs has taken sick and now two little African boys have assumed his role. But as of midday I have not seen them, and thus lay here without food and water covered in my own filth. Me, the Chief Boatswain, powerless, trapped and alone, just like those poor, miserable wretches chained down below in the hold. And like them, I wonder whether or not I will live through this ordeal with the sea. Will I ever see from the bow of the *Henri Real* the beauty of Marseille as it rises up from the harbor on the Mediterranean as the ship approaches the harbor's entrance? Oh, I don't want to die like this...

16 February 1801 – Boatswain, Pierre DuSable, aboard the *Henri Real IV*

No entry for the last two days. The two African boys have not come since almost three days ago. No one comes. My strength dissipates, and my bloody stool only makes me weaker. The sight in my left eye is more blurred than before, and I am beginning to develop jaundice in addition to what has become the pox. I pray to God that death will be swift, and that in the absence of a priest that Mother Mary and all the Saints will forgive me of my sins. And of all the sins it is this reprehensible one of stealing humans and selling them like property. I wonder if this is my punishment for those many voyages I signed on to but should have had the Christian will to avoid. Yet greed, the adventure of sailing and seeing foreign places, and the power over others made me deny my Christian beliefs in order to serve Mammon and its handmaiden, the Devil. Now, as I lay here too weak to call out, sit up or leave this bunk, I see I must pay the ultimate price for my transgressions against the humanity of those who are really my sisters and brothers in God. For those misdeeds I am truly sorry…

As the last breath leaves my body I pray: …*Holy Mary, Mother of God, pray for me, a sinner, in the hour of my death…*

* * *

William

To have been taken from my home and my family is horrifying enough, but what is worse is then to be put aboard something that I knew very little about and chained to others down in the dark, crowded hold of a monstrosity of a boat. The sounds of that boat creaking as it moves through the water, and the total darkness make it seem like a nightmare that I would hope to wake from very soon. Seeing others around me covered with rats and catching whatever disease prevalent down in the hold, makes me wonder when and if the rats will come for me or whether or not I will be affected by the disease and have enough strength to fight them off.

The smell from not being able to wash myself as I did daily back in the village, and the vomit from those who are constantly seasick, compounded by the rats and human waste are stiflingly breath-taking. My state of mind is not as balanced as it should be given these frightfully sickening conditions: death disease, darkness, and the endless moans and cries from the women and children on the above deck as the white crew members forced themselves upon them night after night. This heinous fate that I and others are confronted with forces me to cry out for death – for death to come and wake me from this nightmare so that my soul may make its way back to Mother Africa and home to my village in the cliffs up stream from Ife.

The remembrance of home, my culture, traditions, beliefs, ceremonies, and family are the things that could keep me holding on to life through all the horrors and terror of this voyage through the Middle Passage. If I survive I will probably resemble the walking dead, emotionless, withdrawn, but still trying to comprehend the WHY of my predictament.

*   *   *

Cecilio

On board the ship we are put into its hold below deck, and beaten and subjected to some of the worst living conditions. The heat is unbearable and some die from heat exhausttion. The stench of the dead and sick grow putrid with each day, compounded by the smell of unwashed bodies covered in their own excretion, and is an attraction to the many rats that roamed among us in search of food. I lay in my tight space and wondered what I or the others might have done to deserve such a fate as down in this dark, rat-infested, smelly hold of a ship. Had I transgressed against the gods or the ancestors? Have I sinned against the clan and thus am being sent away to another land in chains? What did I do to end up down here with vermin picking at my open wounds while I sleep?

I continue to bear the lashes from the whips of the pale foreigners and listen to the cries of the women and children beaten as well and ravished by our oppressors. Neither women nor children or any human should be subjected to such terror from other humans. Slowly I begin to see that it's not the gods or the ancestors that punish us but that these pale ones simply wish to do harm to us for their own personal amusement. Is this a given characteristic of the pale foreigners? Is it that they fear that which they do not know, and therefore hide such fear behind the abuse and torture of us?

I soon come to the conclusion that these terrorizing conditions aboard this demon ship can only be stopped through death. It was something I fought to avoid in hopes of waking from this nightmare to live again as I did in the village on the flood plains of Djenne. I now call upon death to come and be my friend in suicide as I end this unbearable pain to body and soul. I die...but my spirit lives on. For me death is a new beginning...

* * *

Matt (1)

To endure the unendurable, that is what an African faces in the depths of a slave ship. To be ripped from your homeland, abducted, and taken away by foreigners who you have never seen before is terror, that is fear. One day you could be eating with your family while the next would be the last time that you ever saw them again. It is unthinkable that one human could subject another to such terror, but in fact it occurred. There were those responsible, but as to whether or not they were ever *held* responsible for those horrible deeds is the question.

Once aboard the slave ship, the African had to face some of the most heinous crimes against humanity ever perpetrated by so-called civilized men. Death shut the eyes, disease racked the body leaving open, infected wounds, rape killed the body and the soul, while beatings bruised, flaying flesh already inflamed by shackles and chains that bound. The hold's deck was littered with human waste, uneaten gruel that fell from weakening hands, and rats and other vermin roaming freely in search of food. The air was stale, filled with the smell of death and others associated with such extremely unsanitary conditions. Entombed in the darken belly of the ship, and subjected to such atrocious living conditions, one option of escape was suicide by starvation or with a successful leap from the ship into the jaws of the schools of sharks that forever shadowed the ship across the Atlantic.

*   *   *

Sarah

I am terrified, and I have lost my humanity as one of many trapped down in this dark, smelly, damp hold of a ship. My freedom has been taken from me and I will never be free as I was in my village there in the Futa Jallon. What is there down the road for me? I am terrified at the prospect of rape by these foreigners who are without color and have a peculiar smell about them. While the children were dancing above on deck in the open for exercise, there was not the slightest indication of hope for a future in their eyes. It is as if they ceased to be children, stripped of their innocence, robbed of their humanity.

Me, I am at a loss as to why this is happening to me. What transgression did I commit against family and the gods to warrant this fate? When we are forced to dance I try to use it as a means to break free from this mental constraint if not the physical. But the only solution to breaking free is death if the opportune time arose. Death would mean my soul breaks free from this earthly body and makes its way back to Futa Jallon, back to Mother Africa.

I pray for death...but as well I pray for life and another day to perhaps reach the end of this journey. As an interlude in these hellish conditions, a sliver of hope strengthens as well as unit us as we detect fear in the eyes of our captors. Do they fear us for who we are: people with color and determination? Or is it a fear that comes from deep within of a hidden feeling of inferiority? With this sign we think revolt; a means to freedom and a way to stop the plundering of the innocence of the children and women. But their weaponry and vigilance douses that hope for the moment. We have to be more vigilant than they for that appropriate opening to strike.

Back down below in the dark of the hold and all its foul smells, I retreat into myself, alone in my cramped space, and once again chained like an animal. I no longer care if I live or die, nor is my body no longer mine. These monsters are upon me and I cannot stop them. My eyes have seen hell, the torture, the terror that comes in the actions of the pale foreigners. I will no longer go silently to my nightly death at the hands of these pale ones. I will cry out in my soul for salvation.

As I cry out I feel my soul leave my battered body. I have gone to a place where I no longer feel the whips, the hands of the ship's crew exploring my body, or the sound of rats rushing across the deck while others eat away at my flesh. I no longer inhabit the hold of the ship. My soul is now free, free to join with those who went before me. Free to go home…home to Futa Jallon and my village deep within the forest…

*   *   *

Treasure

For many days and nights, too many to count, I have lain chained next to people who I cannot communicate with or understand. The only things bonding us together are our skin color, the chains around our wrists and ankles, and the common fear of not knowing what the end of this horrible journey holds for us. All that is certain is that life as we knew it is gone, and Africa, our home, will never be seen again. Soon we will be forgotten, only returning home after death.

Night after night I hear the moans and groans of the hundreds of people tightly packed into a space meant for a fraction of the amount crammed into the space. For a handful of nights I have lain next to a dead person, not knowing if she died from disease or suicide. This cold body next to me is not the only thing I suffer to lay next to. With no room or place to do my bodily functions, I lay in my own waste and the waste of others that spill over into my space. Twice while on this ship I have menstruated which only added to the filthiness that I feel. I lay in my vomit, waste, and menstrual blood, having rats and mice crawl over me, drawn to me by the stench. The smell of this place grows unbearable, with the heat only magnifying the intensity of the stench.

The fact that I am a woman on this ship makes me a target for constant sexual abuse. Every other night I have been snatched from this lower deck and taken above to the room of some pale man of status on the ship and repeatedly raped. If I resist I am beaten as if I have greatly disrespected him. Tired of being beaten, I choose to simply lay there and cry, waiting for him to finish his deed. The chained African men appreciate when night falls because they can sleep and dream of being home. Nightfall for me and the other women means only the continuation of my dehumanization. Before I was captured, I was a proud Ashanti woman with all the potential for being a good wife and mother. Now I don't know who I am or who will have me.

I have watched my fellow Africans be beaten almost to death for no apparent reason other than to instill fear in we captives. I have watched the sick be thrown over-board only to be eaten alive by the sharks, turning the dark sea red. I have seen the dead thrown overboard without any regard for them being people. They are now dead and therefore useless to those who have taken us aboard this ship in chains.

I want to throw myself overboard to end my suffering but because of the wounds at my ankles made by the shackles and my lack of strength, I am too weak to take my own life. I remain at the mercy of these pale foreigners that look like death itself. I just pray that my ancestors will have mercy on me and take me away from this. I want to go to sleep and never wake up…to be reborn and back home in Africa where I didn't know pain like this and had a reason to live…

* * *

Brain

In the days that I have been down here in the dark, I wake in hopes that it is an awakening from this nightmare …an awakening in the embrace of death. I go to sleep nightly hoping and praying that I will never see this horrible world again. I try to convince myself that this isn't real…can't be the world of the living. Here, in the bottom of this ship hundreds of us are packed so tightly that there is hardly room to move or stretch, let alone sit up. The stale, rancid air is breathtaking. We are slowly dying of suffocation.

I have lost count as to how many days this ship has been out on these rough waters on a course destined for a place that exceeds our knowledge. It has been some time now since they last brought us food or water. Before, it was an occasional small portion of food and a splash of water upon our faces and bodies. We had to make do with that and hope against all hope to not become dehydrated. I attempt to satisfy my hunger through sleep and dreams of home. When you sleep hunger pangs subside, the pain of watching others commit suicide are transposed to dreams of them at work and play, and the pain of endless beatings from our ghostly captors drifts away into shouts of joy as I rush across the village commons to collapse into the embrace of family members. But I wake, once again, to the horrors of the ship's hold.

People continue to die and the smell of death is in the air: in our nose and mouth, in our pores. There is nothing I can do to stave it off; and as well I am helpless to ward off the giant rats that feast on the dead. The screams and moans of the sick and weak, whose open sores and wounds attract the vermin, are deafening. Voices cry out for death while others plea for assistance. I contemplate the possibility of taking my own life...escaping this never ending, howling dream. It is a dream in which the cries and wailing of the children and women being ravaged by crew members forever pierces the heart like a lightening bolt. It is a dream in which diseases are evil spirits from the underworld, come as emissaries of the pale ones to steal our souls so that they never return to Mother Africa... never to roam again on the high plains above the rift.

The crew members are coming down more often then before. They cover their mouths and nostrils with linen to ward off the diseased air as each dead body is methodically unchained and carried above deck to be thrown into the sea. Some who are alive but with evidence of disease, they, too, are carried up and thrown screaming overboard to the sharks. They pray over their fellow crew members who *are buried at sea* but not us who are simply discarded like accumulated trash.

I lie in my space and ask what is it that they want from us? Where are we being taken? Is what I am experiencing real or is this that never ending nightmare? The pain that I and the others are going through really cannot be understood by those not caught up in it. Many more of us will have died before this ship's final destination is reached. These inhuman acts upon our humanity by the pale foreigners can only incite anger. It makes me, despite my weakened condition, want to kill myself but at the same time stay alive to help my brothers and sisters. If I could muster the strength and the opportunity presented itself, I would not hesitate to try and kill each and every one of them on this ship! But that is impossible…the nightmare continues…

*   *   *

Matt (2)

I look back across the lands I've called home all my life. The wind moves across the ocean and breaks on my face as I stand in a line waiting to board a ship I have never seen. White men strip me of my brass and copper ornaments, and they burn my back and chain me to the man in front of me. Once below deck, the only sound breaking the silence are the waves that occasionally break against the bow of the boat. We are crowded into what is really too small and dark of a space for our numbers. A sense of loss and desperation hangs heavy over us in the dank air. The constant restlessness of the crew *showed us that they did not know how to stay still and let things be in universal harmony.*

Several days out from land and the sickness begins. The air smells of vomit and body waste. The rats have become comfortable. They circle around us and chew at will. *…so darkness grows into darkness…* The screams from above deck rain down on us as the night goes on. The women and children are raped by the sailors. We lay chained and helpless, unable to save them. I try to close my ears to the horrific screaming but it cuts through the darkness as if to shatter my eardrums. I can only imagine, in this darkened hold, the terror perpetrated on their bodies and souls.

I and others begin to call upon the spirits for help, and we find that through dance, when we are above on deck, the ancestral spirits move through us as we dance in defiance of their orders to dance to their evil music. We find escape…but only for a moment. The ship is our reality for the duration of this journey. And back below we once again are confronted with that reality: little food or water, with time that is non-existence, and day and night are one. In this interminable state suicides double and the surface of the ocean is littered with the dead as ravenous sharks rip them apart.   …*while the rest of us endure the unendurable* I ask spirits that appear, *are you here to accompany the souls of the dead?"*

We are above deck today out in the open air and can breathe cleanly again, at least for awhile. The sun hides behind the clouds in the distance on the horizon. The air is crisp and clean. All is a beautiful sight to behold. In this moment it is so peaceful for us. But in another moment it is gone, and we are once again faced with reality in the hold… but with a realization that comes to us. These pale foreigners fear us. We began to look deep into their evil eyes. There was a fear that lurked deep within their souls, and it sparked something inside of us – a hope, a change. It was a strength that we possessed all along. We are stronger than they, and they know it. They hide behind their weapons of pistols and swords but we lay chained, weak and weaponless. Yet nevertheless that fear of theirs increases daily.

Night, the great healer, watches over us… The night ends as the day breaks in. Twenty more die. Their souls felt trapped below deck as they fought to free themselves. The foreigners believe that the ship is cursed, so they call on their God for help. Who is this God they speak of? Is he not our God as well? Do we die differently from them? Do we not die the same?

It was indeed the driest of all seasons. They came for me. I have been sick for days now, and the sailors have taken notice. I wrestle with the last bit of energy that I have in my soul. They want me overboard, sent to a watery grave at the hands of the most evil of men. I fight, but it is no use. I hit the water after having been thrown from the ship, and am too weak to attempt floatation. As the ship fades in the distance, beyond the horizon, I am alone as I have been all the while on this journey. The fins of the sharks begin to circle and the water is becoming turbulent from their movement. As they approach I hear the faint voice of Mother Africa: *We, Africans, understand the mysteries of life. We were born under the sign of the serpent, and now we must die…but we will be reborn again.*

*   *   *

Dana

To understand what took place on these waters five days out from the estuary and the swirling waters of the Volta that empty into it, is beyond anything imaginable. It was like only yesterday that I saw the tall boat with large fluttering white sails appear off the coast on the horizon. Those on board are French, who after buying us from the interior slave raiders, burned our flesh with white hot iron, and then ferried us out to board and be put down in the dark hold of the boat.

In the hold we were 600 in a space structured for half that number. It reeked of foul, unhealthy odors, and the moans and wailings from those chained, both adults and children, were deafening. The heat was oppressive, with very little air circulating once the hatch was closed. We were entombed, and wondered in horror what would be our fate: are we to be fattened and eaten? What had we done to enrage the spirits of the ancestors? On the second day out seventeen were discovered dead, having died of broken hearts. When we were up on deck yesterday and in the act of dancing for exercise, fifteen others successfully leaped to their deaths into the sea. It seems to be the only way that the soul can be free of these hellish conditions.

As the crew move among us they search for those who show signs of disease, and to prevent its spread remove the infected, though alive, and carry them above to be pitched into the shark-infested waters. Has the world as we know it been turned upside down? Are these pale ones the reincarnation of evil…agents of the devil? Our fury feeds on spilt blood and salty tears. In this upside down world, I find myself alone and friendless, without the protection of the ancestors, and never to see home again.

Others like me have lost all hope that we will survive this tortuous journey. We no longer care if we live or die, but we continue to hold onto the belief that when death does come we will be reborn…

*   *   *

Isaiah

To take a person's freedom away and he not be able to see his family again, is an inhuman act. Me, I know I am not going to survive this ordeal given how well we royalty live in the chieftaincy in comparison to the average villager. I am used to a luxurious lifestyle where food, drink, clothing are in abundance, and attended to by servants.

The food down in this filthy, smelly hold of the ship is ill-tasting, there are worms in it, and the drinking water always has a scum floating on top. The air is damp and stuffy down here, and the place is crowded with chained bodies crying out for this or that – mostly for lost family members and ancestral assistance. One mother holds her hand over her infant child's face to prevent it from breathing, so that it may die and the soul free to return to its village out on the plains of the Akan. Me, I am at a loss as to how this has become my fate. What did I do to deserve this great evil? My spirit is broken, my body damaged in this sea of the living-dead, where vermin of all kind scurry over us and around us spreading disease.

As I lay in a space not fit for the living let alone me, royalty, I hear the spirits of the ancestors tempt me with death…let go…let go… Yet I hesitate as a light flickers within, sustaining me, strengthening my will to live in this hell…in spite of an ancestral call. My palms are moist; my thoughts scramble to keep me sane. My dreams leave me. They have abandoned me to the evil of this hold that is my tomb, though I live… If I can organize my thoughts perhaps the place where our ancestors go might make room for my coming. And, if I can get myself to love the nights in order to prevail, maybe then my lost children will come for me so that I can flee…from here…to a land where the rats don't scurry about over us, where I can cleanse myself of this horrible stench, and together we can sit in the shade of the baobob tree and talk about the wealth of food served us... I die but I die to be reborn… Children, where are you? Hurry!

*   *   *

PART IV – A Shard of Evidence: A Page
from his Diary (Pierre Toussaint)

A Shard of Evidence:
A Page from His Diary

30 January 1801 – Head Cook, Pierre Toussaint
aboard the *Henri Real IV*

Things appear to have quieted down. There isn't the rush of souls, shouts, screams of agony from the wounded and dying that seem to be everywhere on this ship during the night. Somehow the black devils freed themselves from the irons and went against us in a surprise attack. It was probably one of those winches that the men bring up from below at night to have them service their sexual needs who stole the key to the irons. Or it could have been from among those African children who move freely about this ship in, supposedly, well defined work roles. Whoever it was planned it well and when we lest expected such would happen. I hope the souls of those we killed burn forever in hell.

They caught me off guard in the galley. I thought the knock was those two African boys but when I opened the door there stood the blackest beast of a man I ever saw this side of France, and the two boys were with him and holding cutlasses. Fortunately I had my pistol with me and fired it right in the face of the man. He went down fast but not before opening a huge gash in my left side from his cutlass. The two boys came at me as I withdrew further back into the galley, after dropping the spent pistol and grabbing the battle axe from the starboard side of the gallery. It was easy to dispatch them after we three danced about the galley in search of an appropriate opening for the death thrust or to bring my axe around and down on

African captives topside aboard the captured bark *Wildfire* in
Key West harbor, April 30, 1860 (*Harper's Weekly*).

the two of them. I beat them both to it, splitting their heads as one would a pumpkin. But the wound in my side bleeds most profusely; and if I don't remove myself from this bilge and its horrid stench in order to get help, I will surely bleed to death. Yet I am not sure how safe it is to leave...no one has come in search of the cook...

31 January 1801 – Head Cook, Pierre Toussaint aboard the *Henri Real IV*

During the night there was commotion so unlike the normal movement of crew in about the decks of the ship. I still am not sure whether or not it is safe to leave or call out for help from this bilge. Besides, I have bled so much during the night that I grow weak and light headed. Oh, what possessed me to sign up for this voyage? Such slave revolts and attempts at them have been a curse of these voyages for the longest, and on each trip crew members say many Hail Mary's in hope that such a revolt of the cargo never occurs. Sooner or later, we all knew that our luck would run out as it has for me on this voyage. I lay here with my life force flowing out of me, and too frighten and weak to leave or cry out for help.

Before the day is over and night falls again, it is most likely that I will be dead, and how ironic, at the very hands of those whom we sought to use to feather our pockets and the bank accounts of the ship's financiers. Like those Africans who died fighting for a lost freedom, I will soon be food for the sharks...an unfortunate end for one who had hoped one day to captain such a voyage and with the rewards live the life of Louie XIV on a Paris estate... But, I must die the death of one frightened by the deadly actions of those whom we held against their will, either with the use or threat of the very violence whose end result now drains my body of its life force...

Kimberly

Down in the dark, dank, hold of the ship with the worse smells I've ever encountered, I feel nothing but terror and confusion. I am alone...yet with so many others like me chained down to the encrusted, filthy planks of this lower deck. I shake all over while trying to figure out how I came to this state of affairs. Who were those who raided deep into the highlands to snatch me from the village garden? Why me...what did I not do that day to please the ancestors? I poured the morning libations, and put the offering of maize flour in its proper place in the spirit hut. So what did I not do or what did I do wrong? Will these demons who bought me and chained me to this ship return me to my people, or am I to be carried in this vessel to the home of these pale demons to be eaten? Will I be reborn and my soul to wander once again on the bountiful plains of the homeland?

On this ship we females are raped repeatedly by the white crew members. We are handled worse than an animal – we are nonhumans; things to be used, abused and then discarded back down in the hold, only to be brought up again once night falls upon the water. This violation of my humanity is only compounded by the breathtaking smells of human waste, the droppings of the vermin that are as numerous as the cargo, and the stench of the dead that lay among us in the heat for what seem like days.

In my depressed state of mind I pray for death. I refuse food, water and grow weak, so weak that I cannot climb up to the upper deck in the air where they make us dance for exercise. Because I cannot climb to the upper deck, I lose the opportunity for an opening in our captivity to leap to my death into the sea. I lay, therefore, in my bloody body fluids much too weak even to move. My body begins to grow what appear to be sores that soon ulcerate...I have contracted the pox and know that my fate will be the sea.

Soon the pale ones, on their rounds, in discovering my horrible condition unchain me from my space, drag me violently up from what was my tomb to the main deck. The air is moist with morning fog, shrouding the ship in a funeral mist, and the pale ones as pall bearers toss me unmercifully from the aft of the ship into the cold waters. As I hit the water and was pulled quickly under by the large swirls of the sea, I find myself back in the highlands of the Futa Toro weeding the village garden with my baby strapped safely to my back…

* * *

Tatiana

I am terrified of these alien-looking, white men, and am at a loss as to where they are taking me and the others. Why would Africans want to kidnap us and then trade us to these aliens for what appeared to be cloth, trinkets, beads and iron bars? Why was I taken along with the others? What wrong had I committed in the village or against the gods? I have been stripped of my culture, pride, dignity, placed down here in this evil of all evil places by these men with no color, and probably will eventually have to take on aspects of their devilish culture. I cringe at such a thought… But, what ultimately will be my fate once this voyage ends? I am frightened of what lies ahead…

So alone, I am so alone here among these others with languages that sound like mine but are different. Communicating is difficult. When there is light from the open hatch, I anxiously look about for members of my family or village members. None was with me on the long march from the interior to the coast, nor when we boarded the ship. I did not see them in the large crowds. I continue to look feverishly about the hold but with no success, and finally conclude that I will never see them again, not in this life. I have lost an important, life-sustaining force! I contemplate a way out from this hell-hole: suicide by drowning, starvation, or mercifully in the clutches of a deadly disease. The fact that my personal hygiene steadily deteriorates daily, adding to the putrid conditions to which we are chained, means that I could die a psychological death of mental and physical cruelty at the hands of these white, evil aliens.

I die both a mental and physical death...but in hopes of liberating the soul from the pains of such a death...

* * *

Fatima (African, pregnant with child)

There were the cries of newborns reverberating around me over the past few days. The pale of skin have not attempted to take the babies from the mothers. Now it is my turn, and my water has broken here in the dark, and the baby is in the birth canal. The pains of life are, I am sure, so unlike those of death in whose throes many are caught at this very moment that I am about to give life. The pain of the child moving through and out of me is breathtaking but I breathe...breathe deeply and push...push down to help the child into this hellish world in which I am trapped. Oh, the pain of life!

The village women aren't here to assist me and perform the rituals of birth, so I, in my tight space and chained to the ship and the two dead women to my right and left, bite the cord, perform the ritual of new life, and patiently consume the baby's placenta. It momentarily strengthens and gives me hope of a better tomorrow, if not for me the child. But that is hope against all hope...

The child cries and I feed it with the little milk that is in my breast. The trauma of capture and the conditions in the hold have affected my milk, I grow dry and there are no other women who can give their milk. The child cries incessantly and there is nothing I can do. The aliens hear the child when they are among us but make no moves to take it from me. I grow weak and sickly from having given birth and not receive the best of post-natal treatment or given the cleanest of conditions. My body burns with fever…I must have an infection deep inside me. I lay here in my body waste that is also on the baby, and I hold her as close to me as possible to shield off the chilly mist that moves over us when night falls. Yet to no avail and she also becomes sick, and her small body shakes unmercifully…

I know I am dying and soon they will come for me. I put my hand softly over the baby's face to quiet her and take her away from the pains of death – though it was another pain that gave her such a short life – so that her soul might find mine back in the highlands above the muddy river that rushes down to the sea. There we will meet as mother and daughter under the big village tree with family, villagers and elders all to welcome us home...

I rest her quieted, little frame on my chest, call upon the ancestors, and fade into unconsciousness…

*   *   *

Araba

I awoke from my faint and found that we had been packed under the deck of the ship, 600 down in a space built for 300. We had become commercial goods for sale to the highest bidders. It was a process in which the Africans captured or stole us from our village and families, and traded us for material goods to white foreigners who traveled the world in big boats upon the water. This was a business where the whites wished to maximize their investments. I and the others were an important variable in that investment.

The white foreigners have no qualms about dealing commercially in humans. For them it is simply *us* and *them*: they believe they are the better of the two – more superior in all aspects of human behavior. Their involvement, they believed, is a godsend, and the outcome will herald the coming of a place of refuge for the Africans. That place of refuge for the time being is in the unsanitary, unhealthy, and hellish conditions of the ship's hold. Pestilence, sickness and death spare none among the chained humanity: those that are weak, lame, and sick with disease will soon feel the touch of death. Those that do not die below but are alive and diseased are taken topside and pitched into the sea…horrible death…but release and freedom from the horrors of the hold.

Amidst the injustices of the hold, we are forced up to the main deck and made to dance to the tunes of the foreigners. We dance but to the beat of the African drum whose rhythms flow from within us, and we dance as in a trance until the white ones catch on to us. They beat us with whips back down into the hold, men, women and children together. At other times when we were on deck under the night sky with its bright moon and stars, some of those chained preferred the shark-infested waters of the sea to a return to the bowels of the ship. Last night while up on deck, ten of us made it over the railing and down into the dark of the night and into the jaws of the sharks. We who remained on board could not see but heard the splash of their farewells and felt their souls brush pass our faces, caught up in a south-easterly blowing in the direction of Mother Africa. We thought…they will be home soon…

* * *

Shonet

From the moment all of us were gathered on the beach we saw ourselves as slaves, and made even more so as we stood there stripped of any item that was recognizable as cultural. When aboard ship and down in its hold, it was very evident that animals are transported in better and healthier surroundings than we were given, and undoubtedly with more personal space. Space for us was maximized so as to get the largest number of people into an area constructed for a smaller group. Despite the differences in languages and culture, we had become one, but our white captors played up those differences in their attempts to keep us apart.

Our cramped space, bad hygiene or lack of facilities to dispose of human waste exposed the entire cargo to sickness and diseases that were rampant. Those who became sick, contracted disease, or were weakened from refusing food, did not get adequate medical treatment. One had to be strong to survive the horrific, unsanitary conditions that we were subjected to daily. Many thought they were going to be eaten and their bones ground to dust, preventing rebirth back on the Dagon Cliffs high above the plains. Their souls would wander betwixt and between, never able to have the experience of rebirth.

I observe that the pale foreigners pray to their god for safe passage of the ship, which is not so unlike how we pray for mercy to our ancestors and tribal gods. If there is a god to whom they pray, then is it a loving god of its creation as with our gods that watch over all? And if this is so, and we are part of that god's creation, then why do these white ones persecute us the way they do on this ship? Is it that they say and ask their god for one thing and follow the words, but then turn their backs on the god and do wicked things to those of us who have color? Are they just shells of what humans are, but within they are filled with evil and go about terrorizing those with whom they make contact? How long will this hell of theirs down in the ship's hold continue for us, for those who come after us…and on…and on…and on…? One day when my soul and the soul of others will have returned to Mother Africa, will these evil, white foreigners begin to apologize for their centuries of abuse and violence against our humanity? If so, what type of an apology would suffice for such atrocities? Are they capable of such an apology?

I stir as the light from the open hatch cuts through the dark, dank underworld of the hold. Other women around me stir as well and undoubtedly with fear in their awakening. The brightness of the light blinds me momentarily, but as my eyes gradually adjust to it I catch a glimpse of the foreigners as apparitions slowly descending into the hell of their creation, the ship's hold, to begin once again their ritual of terrorizing the helpless human cargo. I wince from the lash of the cat-o-nine tails across my breast…

* * *

Megan

I was going to be a woman. I was beautiful. Mother told me I was going to give babies to one of the boys in the village when I became a woman. In the village…

I can remember a time when the sun would shine on me and dry away my tears. Look at me now. No one could ever want me now. I can see the way the men and the women and the other children look at me when they all know. They can see how I've been touched by the filthy hands of evil. They all know what I have become. Every time those white soul sucking demons come to steal my innocence away, they all just shake their heads in pain for me. They can never do a single thing. They just look at me with shame, pity and sorrow. I've become the whore of the devil. Night after night they use me up and spit me out, back to the depths of hell.

When day comes I have no where to go but the recesses of my mind...but there's not much comfort there. I must be going insane. I scream as loud as I can, but the dead never hear me. I think I'm loosing my mind. I try to fight it but the chains always win, always.

I woke with blood between my legs. In my village, a girl bleeding between her legs symbolizes her entrance to womanhood. My mother was going to teach me the womanly rituals that a woman needs to know in order to ensure that she is clean. In the clutches of these demons I am forever unclean.

I wish the others would stop looking at me like that... I know I'm disgusting. I know I carry the smell of those demons with me. Even a bath wouldn't clean their slime and stench from me, not that I could get one here in this nightmare of a world...

The more death that surrounds me, the more I'm convinced that I am the cause of it. I see faces; faces with pain etched across them. I just need to close my eyes. I almost wish the rats would eat my eyes out... I just want to escape my skin. I need to break out of my skin. Inside this body my soul is still alive, but my filthy body is suffocating my soul.

* * *

Carleen (empathizes and imagines)

I could feel the horror and anguish of those in the bottom of the ship, the darkness that enveloped them, and the terrifying horror of not knowing why, what or how they ended up in such a predicament. What they did know was that they were held down in the ship's hold by men who lacked color in the skin but had evil in their eyes. The unsanitary surroundings were unbearably dehumanizing, conditions ripe for breeding the human epidemics that spread through the human cargo. The ship's hold as well was a haven for vermin, especially large, beady, red eye rats that eat any and everything, living or dead. At night the screams of women and children being violated by the colorless beast of a crew, sent untold terror throughout the lower and upper decks of the hold just above the ship's bilge where the biggest rats secluded themselves. There was nothing anyone could do to prevent that demonic, nightly ritual of lust…

I felt the hopelessness of the Africans while they were down in the hold, but when they were topside that feeling dissipated while they danced to the inner beat of their African drums. Some took the opportunity when it arose, while the white ones were distracted, to hurriedly get up on the ship's railing and jump together into the jaws of ravenous sharks in hopes of a rebirth in their villages on the banks of the Gambia. Death released them from the horrors of the hold.

I felt the strength of those who had the will to live, and all the more so when they realized that the white foreigners, though armed with all types of weapons, feared those who were of color though chained to the ships superstructure. The fear carried a sense of inferiority – that they were not as mentally secure or human enough as their black captives. Aware of this, they preferred to cling to their oppressive, terrorist deeds to hide the reality of their human flaws. I took strength and pride from knowing what the African encountered and had the strength and character to overcome… The African in me is aroused.

* * *

Anthony

As I picture myself as one of the Africans aboard ship, I see bodies on top of one another, with vermin eating at those chained and unable to fight them off. Body excretion is awash on the deck of the hold and laced with blood as many have come down with the flux. The stench is horrendous and very little fresh air circulates in the space filled with the smell of death. Communicable diseases are rampant down in the hold, and those with open wounds are attacked by rats at night while they sleep. The dead and almost-dead are taken topside and tossed into the sea. I cry out to the ancestors for knowledge of why the punishment and where are we being taken. There is no response, only the anguish cries of the women being raped, the screams of those who are tortured for no known reason other than sadism, and the whiny sounds of children lost in a sea of inhumanity.

I as well picture myself as a witness to the atrocities that the whites perpetrate against the helpless Africans, and for what? Is it our color that they lack? Is it our ability to produce children of color and that we are the majority in the world and not them? Do they carry a sense of inferiority under that shield of terror and hate? I ponder these questions as my weak, disease infected body is unchained from the ship's superstructure by the crew members, carried aloft and tossed overboard. Upon hitting the water I hastily let the water pour into my lungs so as to die from drowning in order to avoid the excruciatingly painful tear of the sharks' bite…

*   *   *

Leah – (comments on the proud and brave)

I think that it was probably very frightening to be chained below deck of a ship, especially when one considers its size, most likely very foreign and confusing in itself. It would probably be like some people imagine the abduction of individuals by aliens, who are taken by spaceship to another planet and never to see family and familiar surroundings again. It must have been heart wrenching to know that family members, if among those taken, were to be mistreated by the aliens. I would imagine slave ships to be much like holocaust camps.

Adrift in the middle of the ocean on such a gigantic ship was probably scary for anyone, and even more so while chained to others and breathing stale, putrid air that reeked of death and defecation. To watch and feel those around you dying and committing suicide would not be something I understood or found easy to accept as an escape from the horrors of captivity. The fact of these terrorized Africans having originated from the interior of Africa, and giving of themselves to the sea as a sacrifice (i.e. escape), appears too spiritual for me to venture any thoughts. Their journey through the Middle Passage is just too profound for me at this point to comment upon, except to say they were part of the *many thousands gone* but yet a proud, brave people...

*   *   *

PART V – Up From the Depths:
A Reflective Voice

Up From the Depths:
A Reflective Voice

Angel

It is difficult to place oneself in the position of those chained below in the hold of a slave ship. The captured Africans were branded with a hot iron, shackled, and placed totaling 600 in the hold built to carry a maximum of 300 souls. They were from different tribes in the interior of the coast, and spoke somewhat related languages yet different. That which bound them together was the terror of their imprisonment, and the pressing question as to why/how they were chosen for such a fate.

The experience down in the hold was unendurable. There were suicides as early as the second day out from the island of Goree off the Senegal coast. All around were the odors of unclean, living bodies, and human waste littered the deck of the hold, with vermin of all kinds having free reign across the deck and in among the chained Africans. Very little fresh air circulated in such a small space filled with so many unkempt bodies.

The food was slop, unfit for human consumption, and bits not eaten became part of the piles of filth consumed by the rats, along with all else that littered the deck of the hold. The unsanitary conditions bred diseases in epidemic proportions, and those who were infected and lived, were gathered up with the dead and taken to the upper deck to be unceremoniously tossed overboard. It was a daily ritual to which those left below were witnesses.

The Africans observed the white foreigners carefully and detected restlessness in them that they believed

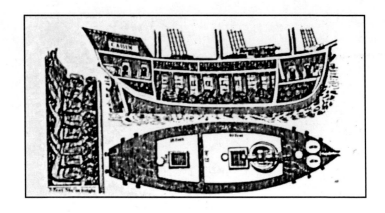

Diagram of a slave ship included in an annual report of the American Colonization Society, 1849, and Logbook of the ship *Catherine* listing deaths of African captives during the Middle Passage between September 1732 and July 1733.

demonstrated a white peculiarity. This peculiarity pointed to the foreigners' inability to accept universal harmony – they wanted to control everything even nature itself. Concluding that it was part and parcel of the predatory nature of these white foreigners, the Africans saw it as driven by fear, the product of perhaps psychological flaws that lay hidden behind a façade of terror and violence left in the wake of their travels around the world.

The Middle Passage, for the Africans was merely an episode in those travels, and was to be the beginning of a long nightmare of atrocities committed against their humanity by those who walked the earth in human form but whose thoughts and actions were those of beasts that walked upright yet with cloven hoofs...emissaries of the devil...

*   *   *

Elizabeth (attempts to envision life down in the hold)

It is unfortunate and disturbing that structural violence of this caliber was allowed to go on for the sake of finding a new means of production. The Manichean psychology allowed Europeans to dehumanize and terrorize Africans. These people were treated like animals and it is hard to imagine being in that predicament.

It disturbs me to watch Europeans beat Africans into submission. It seems like they were conditioning the Africans to fear them. Instrumental violence was an effective tool to conquer numerous tribes at the expense of many African lives. I could not imagine being treated as subhuman and I could not imagine being the perpetrator of such violence. The men who worked on these slave ships must have had a serious psychological flaw to be able to torture Africans. I would be scared not knowing what lies ahead, sick of the never-ending punishment and very pessimistic about my future existence.

If I did not understand my captors' language I would not be hopeful about my destination. The Europeans were indeed a sign of death. I would constantly think about my homeland, constantly wondering if I would ever return home. I think my faith would be the only thing growing stronger in my life, dwelling on my gods and my homeland – Mother Africa. I could not take being torn away from my village or my family. I think I would get lost in memories and would continue to imagine my once happy life. I would be one of those people whose mind completely shuts off. I would be a shell of myself, probably hoping for death. Death would be better than living chained in human waste and vermin. The conditions below the deck were entirely too much to handle. I would welcome the moments of sleep, perhaps my dreams would be the only escape.

I could not imagine living in those conditions. I'm not surprised hundreds of people died when they were packed like sardines in such unsanitary conditions. The smell alone would be entirely too much to handle. The seas were rough and I would be constantly seasick, and contributing to the repulsive conditions below deck down in the ship's hold. Because the Europeans believed Africans were subhuman, they cared less about diseases or sanitations. On top of beatings and torture, Africans had to endure terrible, filthy conditions of festering wounds, human waste, unclean water, unhealthy food in limited portions, and stagnant air, *ad infinitum*. I shiver at the recollection of expressions on the faces of the Africans down in the ship's hold which were so penetratingly frightening. The evil they were confronted with could be felt through their gaze.

Instead of trying to fix sanitary conditions, the sick were tossed overboard to meet their death. I imagine many Africans were sick due to the conditions. For me, I would be thankful having met my death in the sea. After many days at sea I would not have faith that conditions were going to get better. I would not be a strong individual in such a situation. I would not be able to endure for long the conditions, not knowing a soul, and/or saddled with an unclear future.

I would wish the same fate for the Europeans as my own. If only we could trade places for a day perhaps they might realize the atrocities they commit on a grand scale against our humanity. Being a woman I'm sure I would be subjected to endless, sexual assaults, and my whole existence would be changed forever. Just being on the slave ship would have changed me as well, but having to endure violent sex with the European captors would create in me an uncontrollable rage and hatred. I am appalled at what the Africans endured, and shocked that structural violence this great was permitted among so-called civilized nations for centuries.

*   *   *

Orlando (His voice recollecting the horrors of his captivity)

It was frighteningly, dreadful being left below deck with no remorse for our lives. We were taken from our homes, villages, and land, and linked to one another by chains. Many if not all of us were from different places in Africa. We had different languages, religions and cultural aspects, but were brought together by these pale monsters. These monsters, who knew nothing about us or our land, wanted us for their own personal use. How did all this begin for me and the others? It was an indigenous, African slavery but under the pale ones a genocidal slavery of an unending time.

Many of us were sold by kings to the French while others were captured in raids on villages in the hinterland. Before being put on board ship, we were branded and stripped of all personal items. We knew that we would never return to Africa the same, if ever…

On board ship and down in the hold with almost 600 others like me - in a ship whose original capacity was for 300 – we were confronted with inhuman living conditions. Death, disease, and body excretion were everywhere. The hold was unsanitary, unsafe, infested with large rats and other vermin eating at dead bodies and human waste. I, like others, lay next to the dead for what appeared to be hours, maybe days. We were given very little space; perhaps half or less of what one would have received if the capacity of 300 was maintained.

For those who were lucky enough to have died, it was thought they were finding their way back to Africa. As for the rest of us, we had to go up on deck and dance, not because we wanted to but because we were forced to dance for exercise and to entertain the pale ones. There, on deck, we watched the dead (some having committed suicide) and the diseased-living, being thrown overboard to schools of ravenous sharks churning the sea red with blood as they devoured the offerings. We sat there, with no choice other than to wait until it was our time. At night, from below, we had to listen to the pale ones above forced themselves on our women and children.

Time for us was without end. We had ceased to be human. We had become nothing more than breathing property. Some of us thought, why? Why must this happen to us? What did we do to deserve this? But most of us stood strong, sharing language and other aspects of culture. One culture aspect we shared that bound us all was when taken up on deck to dance, rather than dance for the pale ones, we danced to evoke the ancestral spirits.

We felt them move through us, bolstering our stamina and shoring up our will to live.

Those of us who held on to the will to live prayed. for better days or a day that would be better than the one before. This became evident as we began to detect fear of us in the eyes of our captors. Even though we were chained securely to the ship's superstructure, they feared us, and even with their guns, knives and other weapons, the fear was there. Some of us felt this was an opportune time to attempt to overpower them. We fought like trapped beast, valiantly but to no avail. The weaponry of the pale ones carried the day. Many died but it did not matter because for that night we fought back!

When we reached land not our own we were separated between the ones who were skilled enough to work versus those who couldn't. We were sold to other oddly dressed pale ones who ran screaming at us to claim human property they had purchased.

The journey from our own land to one very foreign cost us many lives. The journey opened our eyes to the threat of Europeans (the pale ones), as well as reveal that our own people would turn on us for a little bit of money. After all that was said and done to us, it is no wonder why we are strong and why we hold such close ties with our ancestors, and even the spirits of the land.

* * *

Darvin

My mother was as beautiful then as she is now, but then we didn't know a monster was to come and almost rob her naked. My mother never could have wanted such a destiny for her children. Blinded by darkness as dazzling as the sun, the thief came and took all he could from my mother, my mother Afrika. The filth, disparity, and uncertainty of our conditions made us wonder where this voyage would lead us. The pale foreigners we see are aliens; and it's rather unfortunate that evil crossed our path, for we did not know what was to become of us.

Some of my brothers and sisters die slowly while others are forced to watch how the innocence is taken away from our children as well as be subjected to the cries and painful screams of the women being raped. Diseases in epidemic proportions become our demise, for we are just instruments of use and discard, not humans. The survivors must contend with abominable conditions down in the ship's hold, whose deck is littered with feces, urine, vomit, blood, and with vermin of all kinds, and humans, trekking back and forth over the deck. Are we – the trapped souls entombed in this hellish ship – to suffer this fate so that later generations may be spared this evil perpetrated upon us by the pale ones…the white foreigners who move amongst us like ghosts from hell?

Yet in all of our pain we found unity among the many other sons and daughters from Mother Afrika here in the hold. Together we prayed for death so that our souls could be carried back to Mother Afrika on the wings of the great birds to be free once again in our own land and out of the hands of these white aliens. But hope began to surge in us out of the realization that these pale ones feared us. We could see the fear in their eyes, and it was there even though they had weapons and we none besides being chained to the ship. They feel inferior to us but why, given their weaponry and other technology that powers and give direction to the ship? Is it our color or the way we bear the pain from their violent acts against us? Whatever it is, it presents an opening for us of which to take advantage. It seems that they attempt to suppress their fear by their hold over the women and children through rape, which they feel empowers them. It hurts me deeply to hear the cries of the children and women being raped repeatedly night after night, to the extent that their bodies and souls become numb to the pain inflicted on them by these aliens.

Kings and queens raped my mother, broke her soul but had no idea how powerful she really is. Powerful beyond measure: shackles, chains and whips cannot stop us from trying to escape this fate by committing suicide or fading away in our pain. Where is the hope, where do we look for hope? We're alone and restless down in this hold. And whether I turn left or right, I still see nothing but the mistreatment of my people. We are dying, and not even the strong ones stand a chance to overcome death; and the bodies of the women continue to suffer the rage and anger these aliens inflict upon them when night falls on the ship.

We complete the Middle Passage, and it is a bitter sweet arrival as I start to remember Mother Afrika and all those I was forced to leave behind. Where is the justice? These white aliens came to us as a curse (but for what transgression against the gods?) that will haunt the generations to come. But for now, we must fight to keep the memory and honor of Mother AFRIKA alive in our hearts and souls forever!

* * *

Christian

Footsteps in the dark and the rattling of chains, so began this cruel narrative of "the many thousands gone," sold into slavery to the French by their tribal captors: *more black bodies in a sea of dark despair*. The silence in the ship's hold is deep and penetrating. Bodies lie lifeless and unblinking except for thick beads of sweat dripping down dark flesh.

There were seventeen suicides in the second day. Shackled feet step lively on deck to the sound of cracking whips and a lone violin. Above, great white sails unfurl symbolically. The terror of the first epidemic is unspeakable. Disease ridden bodies are splashed with large buckets of seawater, washing back the vomit and rats. Prisoners are forced to dance while their women and children are repeatedly raped by the white captors. It is said that *once the Manichean psychology takes root in the heart and mind [of the oppressors], it becomes remarkably easy to embark on pogroms, pillage, rape and every other conceivable crime.* The Africans are forced to dance in an attempt to invoke their native gods. Some prisoners escape overboard. *Spirits of the sea be merciful to us.* Alas, those who jumped are soon pulled under by the swirling sea as schools of sharks appear off in the distance. The rest lay stricken with fear down in the depths of the hold, forced to consume their small rations of doughy pulp. Such cruelty visited upon our humanity is institutional violence and is defined as *the infliction of pain and/or injury, or the use of physical constraint in order to induce another person to carry out some action against his wishes.* In this case the oppressed are forced to pursue little action, save enduring their captivity and the fear of bodily harm.

A prayer goes out to the tree of Mother Africa as the prisoners plan their revolt in the rat-infested hold.

It is the interpersonal violence and greed among African tribes that has led to this horrifying exodus. Listen carefully and you can hear the Africans' terrorizing, descriptive wails of the burning and pillaging of their villages and how they arrived in the hands of the slavers. "The many thousands gone"...

As the epidemic spreads on board, living people are flung headlong into the sea. Countless bodies vanish beneath the dark tide with no funeral ceremony of any kind. A revolt in the hold of the ship leaves many more

dead and injured. For those who were consumed by the
ever present violence that stalked the ship, [their] history is
obliterated; [they] cannot control what happens to [them]; [they]
feel victorious if [they] escape an ever present peril.

And what fate befell those survivors who endured
though their spirits and bodies lay in ruin? They emerged
from the filth, maggots and rats to be sold to the whipping
post on American soil.

The Middle Passage is deserted now, and its turbulent
and consuming waters are still, but its history of pain and
turmoil remains. It was a trade route spanning the length
of the great Atlantic. For those whose journey began on
the African shore, many could only find rest at the bottom
of the sea. "The many thousands gone" but whose tale
of the journey reaches out across that time barrier to be
told...in their own words.

*   *   *

PART VI – Figures I & II: Student Responses and a Celebration

APPENDIX 1

Student Response/Reaction to:
In Their Own Words: Voices From The Middle Passage
Historical Terrorism Class Fall Semester 2007

"While reading 'In Their Own Words' I could see in the writings of those who contributed to the story, that they really put themselves in the positions of these men and women. The pain, beatings, rapes, sickness and death that took place on that ship were horrifying…"

—Lisa

"'In Their Own Words' does a great job at recreating the voices of the Middle Passage. Through various stories students' knowledge and empathy of enslaved Africans… is clearly illustrated. The major themes presented in their essays are death, sexual abuse and inhumane living conditions."

—Aries

"It is an indescribable feeling that finds refuge in my stomach when I hear the story spoken from the mouths of those that endured it. For me the Middle Passage is no longer just an elusive diagram of a ship that was once passed around in my middle school social studies class, a diagram which I mistook the placement of bodies for designs"

—Alyssa

"This horrific crime perpetuated upon Africans for the profit of others is vividly recounted in "Voices". We read poignant first-hand accounts of the pain and sufferings placed upon these prisoners."

—Alicia

"We can all see the rats and feces in which these innocent women and children lived. We can even imagine the smells along with the sounds of the moans and waves causing nausea and insanity. Thanks to 'In Their Own Words' we have the privilege of getting 'almost' first-hand accounts of what these Africans went through."

—Derek

"This reading brought out many emotions in me. I have never read a piece so realistic and honest where I could feel the pain, fear, and worries of the slaves...The reading made me gain more respect for the slaves because it shows how strong they were."

—Edlin

"For the most part...chronicling the history of the slave trade is from those profiting from the exploitation of Africans. However, 'In Their Own Words' addresses the lesser known side of the situation: the stories and experiences from the victims' points of view. "

—Katy

"After reading these anecdotes I closed my eyes and tried to imagine myself in a similar position, experiencing the odors, the splintered wood in my back, the cries of pain around me, the feeling of hopelessness and the wait for my impending death. What would I do? Nothing! Nothing is all I could do."

—Katy

"It is very important that we learn more about the personal experiences that Africans went through in order to complement and/or challenge the perspectives of Europeans on the Middle Passage. I believe 'In Their Own Words Voices from the Middle Passage' is a great collection of writings that tells us to see history from another perspective as that offered by 'Voices'."

—Jhokasta

"Each account I read was believable, imaginable, and all the more disturbing than the last. I believe that this is a fantastic way of learning, understanding and growing as a class and as an educated person."

—Katelyn

"In reading 'In their Own Words' I was deeply moved and pained. Suicide was a common theme that really made an impression on me. I cannot imagine jumping to the sharks to free oneself from the terror of living or the physical pain of being chained in a moving prison…"

—Tommi-Grace

"'In Their Own Words' is teeming with imagery, emotion, and life questions. It seems that it is impossible to read such a work without an eruption of feeling, and a necessary questioning of the past and the present. I think the anthology serves to remind us all that while some suffer, no one is free."

—Marigo

"I was very interested in the students' interpretations and various portrayals as they put themselves in the minds and bodies of those held captive on the ship. The term 'psycho-drama' which was used in the article to describe the process which the students used to write their own essays is a very interesting one."

—Shante

"The accounts of people aboard the ship imagined by students, sew together a tapestry that reflects the sheer brutality and callousness with which they were treated and the unbearable struggle of day-to-day existence."

—Michelle

"'In Their Own Words' took me to another time and place. I found myself trapped in a nightmare where words had no meaning, because no one could understand…No one knew me…Even the loudest screams couldn't wake the dead…As I read on…each entry was…a flashback to a time that I never thought I would have to go through again."

—Megan

APPENDIX II

State University of New York at New Paltz
DEPARTMENT OF BLACK STUDIES
A Reading and Viewing in Celebration of the

TWO HUNDRED ANNIVERSARY OF THE
OUTLAWING OF THE TRANSATLANTIC TRAFFIC
IN AFRICAN CAPTIVES
1808 – 2008
23 October 2008
Lecture Center 104
7:15 – 9:30 p.m.

Readings – By students, giving voice to the voiceless from: *In Their Own Words – Voices from the Middle Passage* (a class assignment where students in *Historical Terrorism Against Native and African Americans* and *Black History I* recreated voices for those chained below deck on a slave ship crossing the Atlantic Ocean – the dreaded Middle Passage)

Voices up from the deep
Slave Ship *The Brookes*   **Read by**

Act I – From shore to ship

Rachel	Latosha Belton
Sunday (male age 9)	Rafael Pena
Takeya	Artie M. Williams
Christina	Marian E. Buzon
Unknown female	Arielle Koonin
Ashton	Emily Sussell
Fatima	Katedra Payne

Act II – Resistance   **Read by**

Jacob   Perry Taylor
Darryl   Luis Candelaria
Pierre Toussaint (cook)   Natalie Cespedes

Act III – Afterwards: the Voyage continues

Jennifer   Maybin Martinez
Esperanza   Gloria Viveros

Film – *The Middle Passage*
(Courtesy of Ms. Kimberly K. Henry)